AF752398

ABANDONED EASTERN INDIANA

DECAYING UNDER THE SNOW

AMANDA BENNETT-COLE

AMERICA THROUGH TIME®
ADDING COLOR TO AMERICAN HISTORY

Fonthill Media Inc.
www.fonthillmedia.com
office@fonthillmedia.com

First published 2023

Copyright © Amanda Bennett-Cole 2023

ISBN 978-1-63499-490-3

All rights reserved. No part of this publication may be reproduced, stored in a retrieval system or transmitted in any form or by any means, electronic, mechanical, photocopying, recording or otherwise, without prior permission in writing from Fonthill Media Inc.

Typeset in Trade Gothic 10pt on 15pt
Printed and bound in England

CONTENTS

ABOUT THE AUTHOR

Amanda is based out of Lafayette, Indiana, where she pursues her interests of researching weird local history and recreational trespassing. At this point, she has distinct preferences for every GIS property search system in the Midwest region and will make it known. Besides research and exploring, she uses her free time to play video games, learn horrific vintage recipes, and spend quality time with her family and friends.

INTRODUCTION

My exploring partner, Jenny, and I have loved road trips ever since we were able to drive. Whenever we set out to explore, we have multiple locations mapped out, and we always take the back roads. Exploring Eastern Indiana was no different. On our way to Grissom, we were incredibly lucky with side-of-the-road finds of old houses, schools, and a church. Since we're based in Tippecanoe County, exploring the eastern half of the state led to multiple eight-hour road trips. With the help of Google Maps, we can figure out if the random crop of trees in the middle of a field is hiding an old house (it is around 25% of the time). We've also gotten to go through a number of towns small enough that they no longer appear on maps. Some we have liked more than others. Being able to stop at weird roadside attractions is also a plus, like the Pink Elephant in Fortville or the Largest Ball of Paint in Alexandria. We stop for historical markers on the side of the road and get excited by all the different types of bridges Indiana has to offer. Throughout our exploring, we have learned that Indiana's VFW's tend to have tanks out front, while Illinois typically has planes.

1

GRISSOM AIR FORCE RESERVE BASE

Typically, when we visit military installations, they are completely decommissioned; however, Grissom was an exception due to its history and decline over the years.

Blueprint drafts for what was then called Naval Air Station Bunker Hill were presented in April of 1942. The installation was commissioned July 1, and shortly after, the first group of naval personnel moved onsite. The majority of the field work was finished, but the actual construction wasn't finished until April 12, 1943. The total price came to $13,064,424.43 (equivalent to $225,049,436.60 in 2022). The plan requested a 2,158-acre Navy Air Station to house and train 1,200 naval aviation cadets. This would cover the 3,200 officers and men's housing needs as well as other facility requirements. The station would have seventy-seven buildings, a water supply, heating, sewage disposal systems, four runways, a square landing pad with sidewalls, taxiways, warm-up aprons, and approaches.

The Site Selection Board chose this location because it was proximate to several major cities and was strategically located. The ground was level for miles in all directions, opening a wide range of options for auxiliary fields. It was not on any of the commercial airlines' flying paths. The soil type was suitable, and gravel for concrete could be found nearby. With a station only 1.5 miles distant and the easy building of a switch track, the area could be served by the Pennsylvania Railroad. Paved highways and bus routes were also close by. The only disadvantage appeared to be the water treatment for the steam boilers. (Bragg)

To educate pilots for the United States Navy, United States Marine Corps, and United States Coast Guard, Naval Reserve Air Base Peru was established. During WWII, the base underwent a number of renamings. The name was changed to

Naval Air Station Peru (NAS Peru) on January 1, 1943, and then again on March 1, 1943, to Naval Air Station Bunker Hill (NAS Bunker Hill), which it retained for the duration of the war.

Pre-flight training lasted for twelve weeks, following which the pilot would move to Bunker Hill for another twelve weeks of flight training before continuing their instruction at an intermediate aviation training facility like Naval Air Station Pensacola. Cadets at Bunker Hill learned about celestial and dead-reckoning navigation, radio communication, engine maintenance and repair, and physical fitness training like boxing, wrestling, hand-to-hand combat, and swimming. The installation educated 5,997 American naval aviation cadets, 4,568 of whom were moved to Naval Station Great Lakes for reclassification, while the remaining 854 qualified for advancement to Intermediate Flight Training. Bunker Hill also educated 701 cadets for the British Royal Navy in addition to the American cadets. There were 407 N2S-3 Kaydet trainers as of March 31, 1945, making up almost a fifth of the U.S. Navy.

Ted Williams, a former baseball player in the major leagues, was one of Bunker Hill's most well-known graduates. At NAS Bunker Hill, he trained to become a Marine Corps naval aviator. The installation was deactivated after World War II and converted to agriculture, with a civilian staff of government caretakers maintaining the military structures. (National Park Service)

On November 16, 1951, the United States Navy granted the United States Air Force access to twenty-five buildings as the Korean War loomed, and the site was used by the United States Air Force Storage Branch. On March 31, 1954, the Navy fully transferred it to the Air Force while it was still deactivated. On June 22, 1954, the site was officially transferred to Tactical Air Command and reopened by the Air Force as Bunker Hill Air Force Base. Despite the arrival of the 323rd Fighter Bomber Wing in 1955, no flying took place until the runway was finished in 1956. The base started to house the TAC's Ninth Air Force's 4433d Air Base Squadron, 323d Fighter-Bomber Wing, and 323d Air Base Group. In order to gain proficiency in tactical air operations, North American F-86 Fs were initially used for training before being swiftly upgraded to the North American F-86H Sabre, and finally the North American F-100A/D in 1956. On September 1, 1957, Bunker Hill Air Force Base was handed over to Strategic Air Command (SAC) from Tactical Air Command, and the 8th Air Force was given jurisdiction over the base. The Air Force immediately deactivated the 323d Fighter-Bomber Wing, and the 4041st Air Base Group arrived the same day. In 1957, the Air Force started stationing the brand-new Boeing KC-135A Stratotanker at the site. The 305th Bombardment Wing was transferred by Strategic Air Command from MacDill Air Force Base in Florida to Bunker Hill Air Force Base on June 1, 1959. (National Park Service)

A B-58 bearing five nuclear weapons, including a 9-megaton thermonuclear bomb, skidded off an icy runway on December 8, 1964, while on a military exercise, and caught fire. While turning onto the runway and applying its own power, it got caught in the jet blast of the aircraft in front of it. The bomber lost control as a result and skidded off the left side of the taxiway. The left main landing gear brushed the left edge of a concrete light base before continuing 10 feet over a flush mounted taxiway light fixture. After moving forward another 10 feet, the left main landing gear collided with an electrical manhole box which consequently ruptured a fuel tank. The aircraft then caught on fire. Leary Johnson, the aircraft commander, and Roger Hall, the defense system operator, were able to escape with only minor wounds. They managed to flee rather soon by opening their canopies and leaping to the ground. However, the position of the navigator's seat—in the middle of the other two—made exiting the aircraft much more challenging. And the fire spread quickly because the plane was fully fueled with 14,000 gallons of a highly combustible kerosene-gasoline mixture and was always ready to take off for the Soviet Union. Manuel "Rocky" Cervantes, the navigator, ejected from an "escape pod" while the plane was being engulfed in flames. He was launched 100 feet into the air. There was no time to fill the parachute. The pod impacted the tarmac violently and Cervantes quickly passed away. (Higgins)

The incident was downplayed by the press and the Air Force. For the first time, an Air Force spokesman acknowledged that nuclear weapons were in Indiana, although he insisted on using the phrase nuclear "device." He claimed there was nothing to be concerned about. A twelve-hour fire consuming five nuclear weapons made headlines for just two days. Parts of the five nuclear warheads on board the airplane were burned in the ensuing fire. Despite some of the high explosives melting and burning, the weapons' high explosives did not detonate. One of the burning weapons was taken from the scene and snuffed out by putting it in a small trench and covering it with sand. A different area of the facility was used to excavate and bury the aircraft wreckage and the polluted soil surrounding it. It was claimed that thorough sampling done in the area soon after the accident proved there was no contamination there.

The instrumentation available at the time of the incident (alpha scintillation and Geiger-Mueller detectors), in combination with the moist conditions, raises additional concerns about the accuracy of the delineation of residual contamination with respect to present standards. All around America, Atomic Energy Commission sites received the recovered weapons and weapons debris. Analysis of the wreckage and damaged weapons later revealed that none of the plutonium-bearing components had been damaged, proving that no plutonium had been discharged into the environment.

At Grissom ARB's request, the Air Force Safety Center reviewed the classified and unclassified records it had in its possession in June 1996 and came to the conclusion that there was insufficient information to support the site's unrestricted release. (Rademacher)

In 1968, Bunker Hill Air Force Base was renamed Grissom Air Force Base in memory of the late Lieutenant Colonel Virgil Ivan "Gus" Grissom, an Indiana native, Purdue University graduate, and one of the first seven astronauts to represent the United States of America. (The Air Force Civil Engineer Center)

The military was reduced as a consequence of the conclusion of the Cold War. Grissom Air Force Base should be shut down, according to the Base Realignment and Closure Commission of 1991. In June 1992, the Strategic Air Command (SAC) was deactivated by the Air Force, and the 305th Air Refueling Wing stationed at the facility was transferred to the recently formed Air Mobility Command (AMC). Air refueling planes from Strategic Air Command and strategic airlift planes from the concurrently dissolving Military Airlift Command were combined into the Air Mobility Command (MAC). Grissom Air Force Base was reassigned to the Air Force Reserve in accordance with the 1993 Base Realignment and Closure Commission's directive (AFRES). In 1994, two units (one reserve and one active duty) were decommissioned as a result of changes in the Air Force's mission. Grissom was reorganized as an Air Force Reserve Command facility in October of that same year. Today, Grissom is one of only five Air Force Reserve Command bases in the country, and the host unit is the 434th Air Refueling Wing. Grissom Air Force Base is home to groups from different branches of the American armed forces; however, the Air Force has the largest personnel presence there. Since the 1970s, the Army Reserve has been stationed at Grissom, and in 2001, a Marine Corps Reserve unit transferred there. (The Air Force Civil Engineer Center)

Grissom Air Reserve Base not only helps to defend our country, but it also has a significant impact on the neighborhood. It employs both civilian and military personnel and is the third-largest employer in North Central Indiana and Miami County. It has a yearly economic impact of more than $140 million. The "Toys for Tots" program is just one of the many community initiatives that Grissom units are actively involved in, and the National Arbor Day Foundation named the base a "Tree City."

Due to its 12,500-foot runway, Grissom was also designated as one of the emergency landing sites until the Space Shuttle was retired on July 21, 2011. (The Air Force Civil Engineer Center)

Right: The Grissom Inn, where those visiting the base would stay.

Below: A business sign, including a faded caution sign added after the restaurant fire.

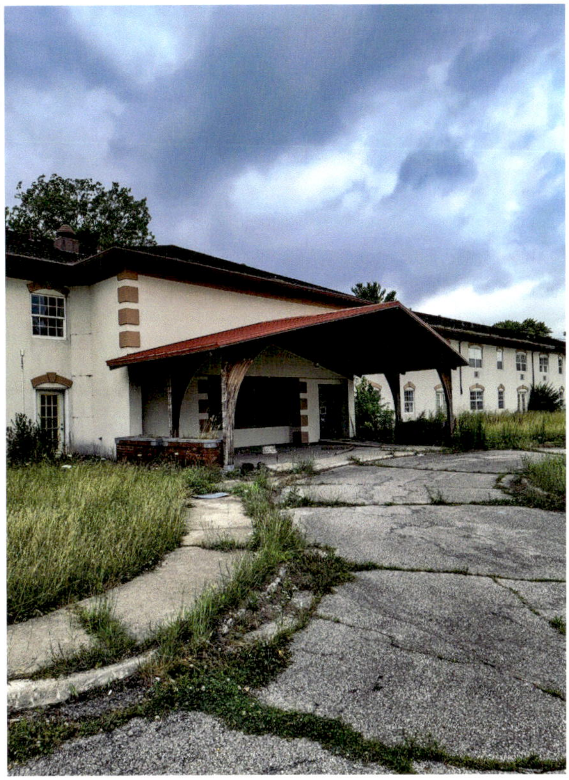

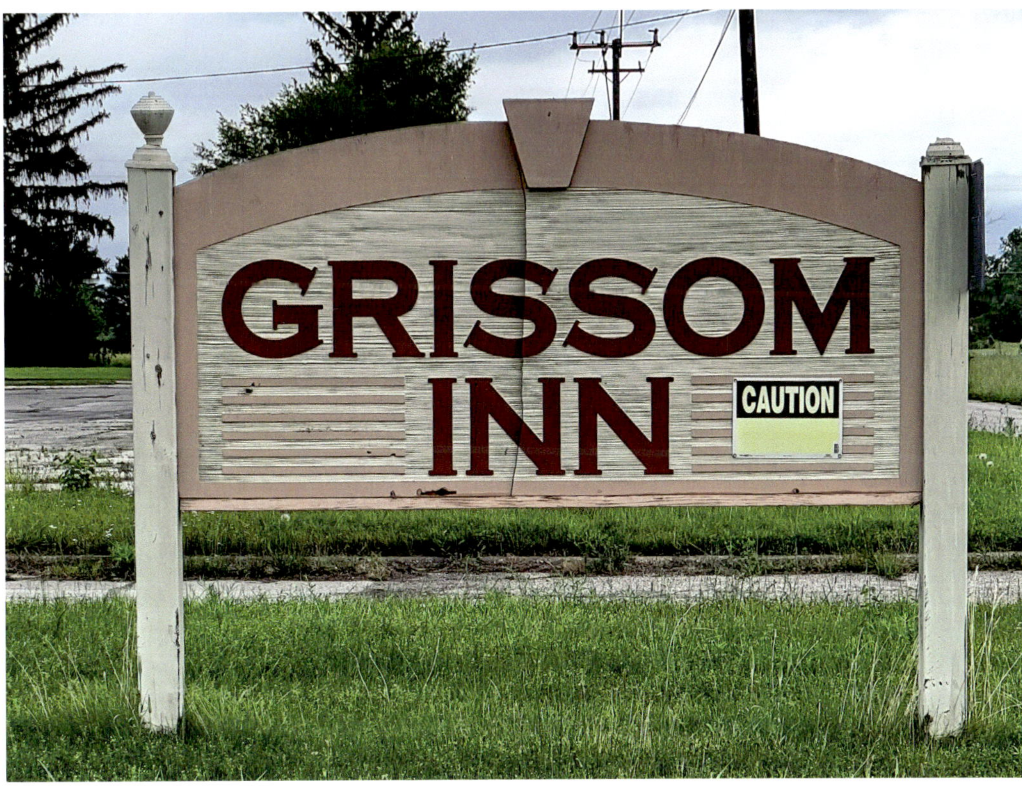

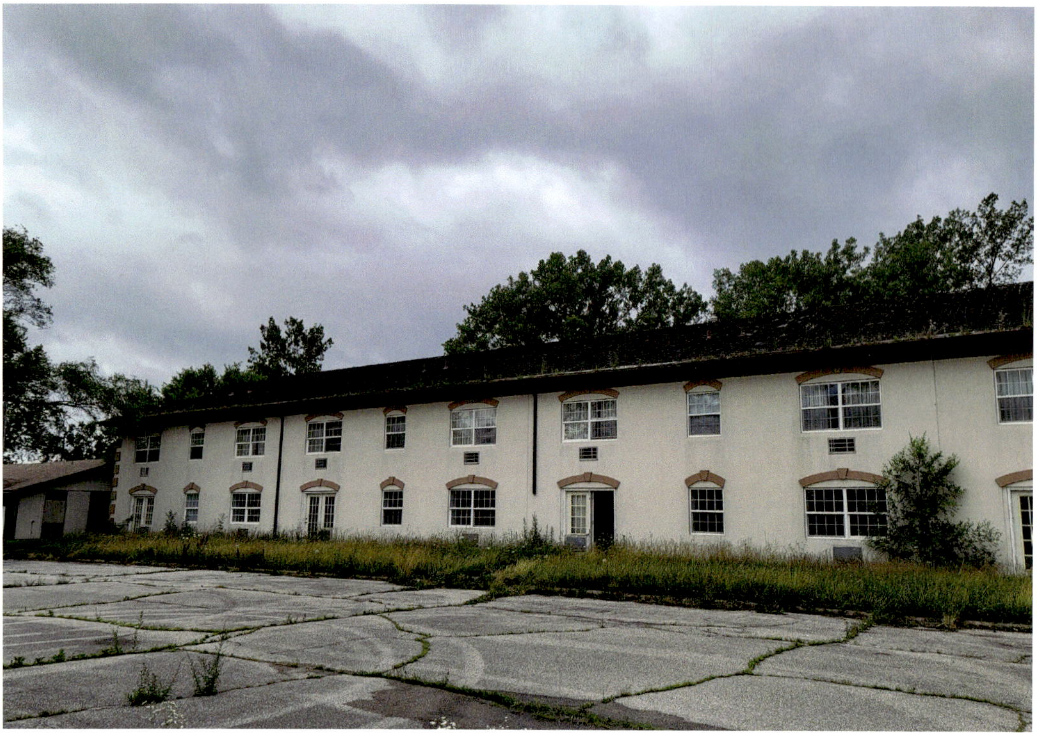

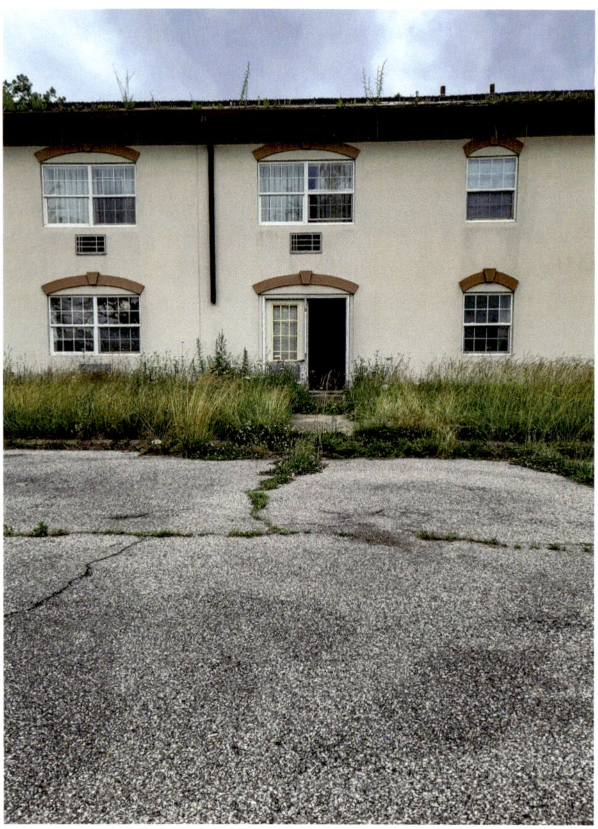

Above: It was very surprising that very few windows were broken and only one door was left open.

Left: Our method of egress.

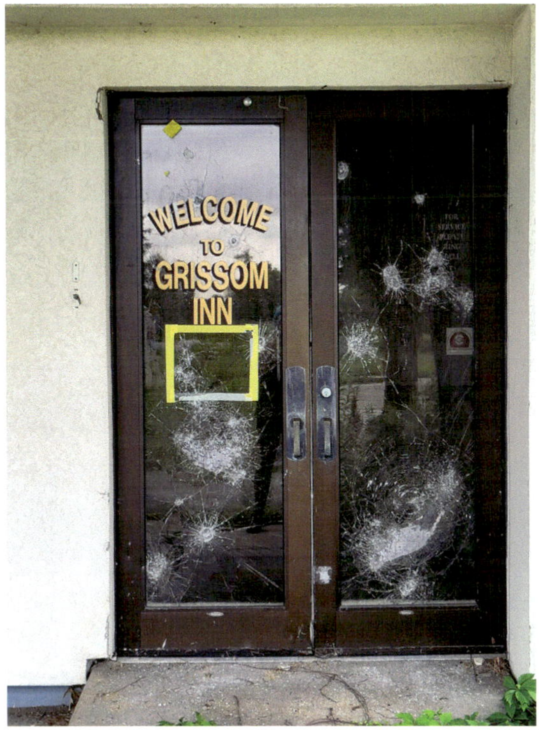

Right: People have obviously been trying to get into the front door through the reinforced glass.

Below: A full shot of the front entrance; the light fixture looks like a repurposed oil lamp.

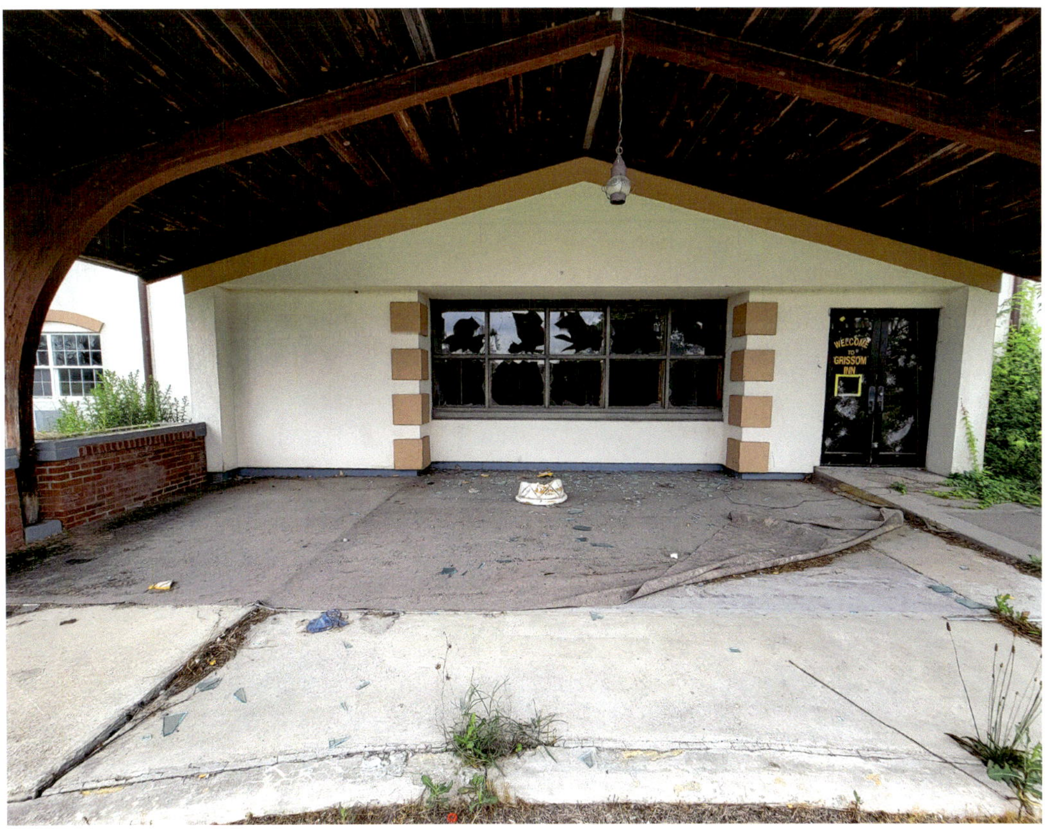

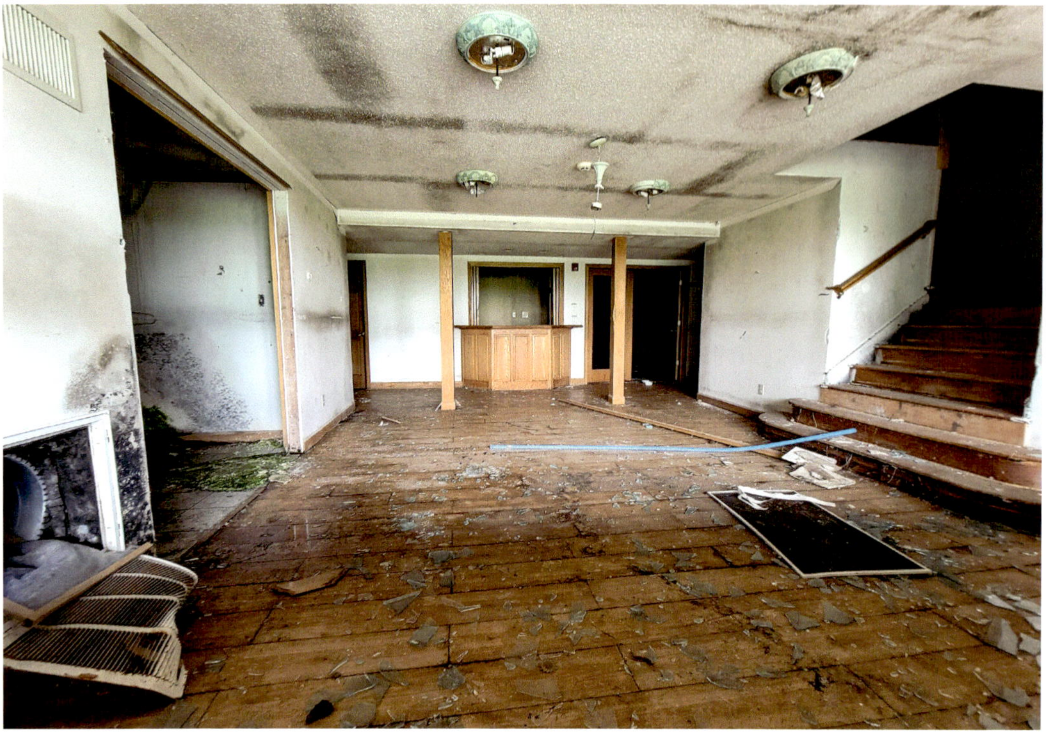

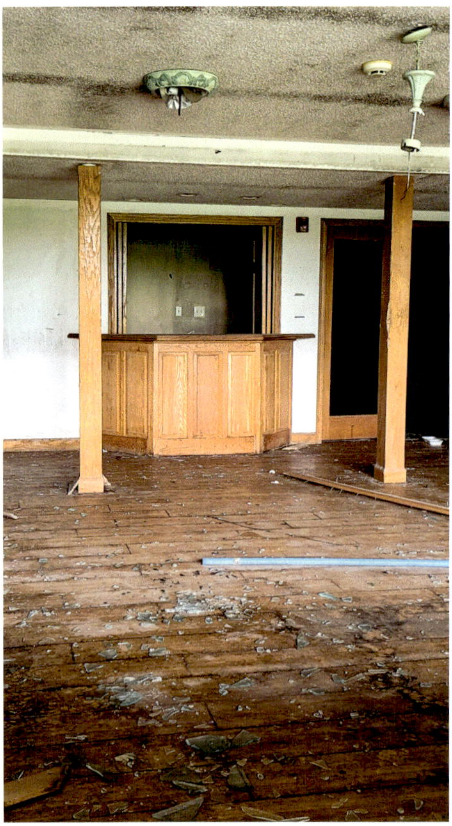

Above: The check-in counter and front foyer. The light fixtures are original to the building, and you can see how the mold has made its way inside.

Left: The check-in counter, plus a closer shot of the remnants of the lights.

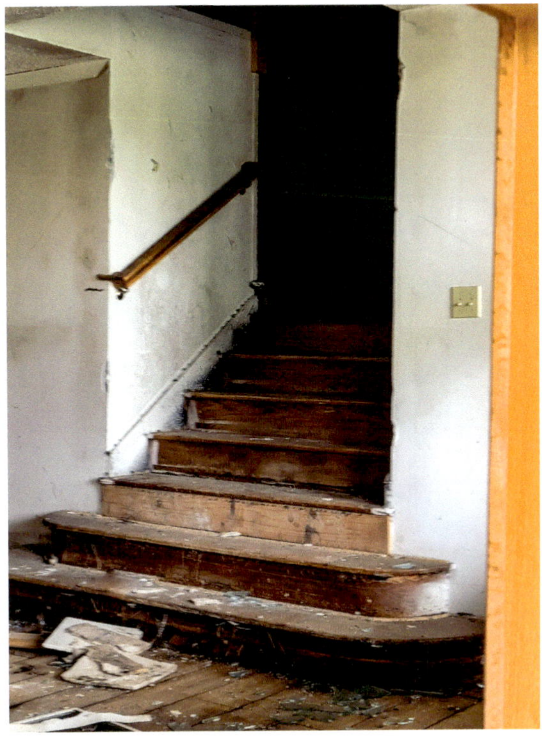

It was interesting that mold started to form on the stairs rather than the wall.

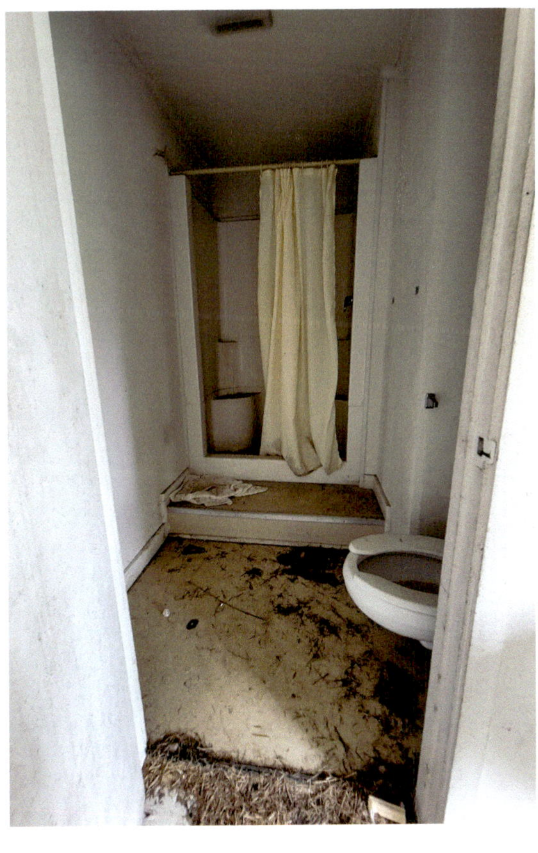

This was most likely an accessible room, as evidenced by the seat in the shower.

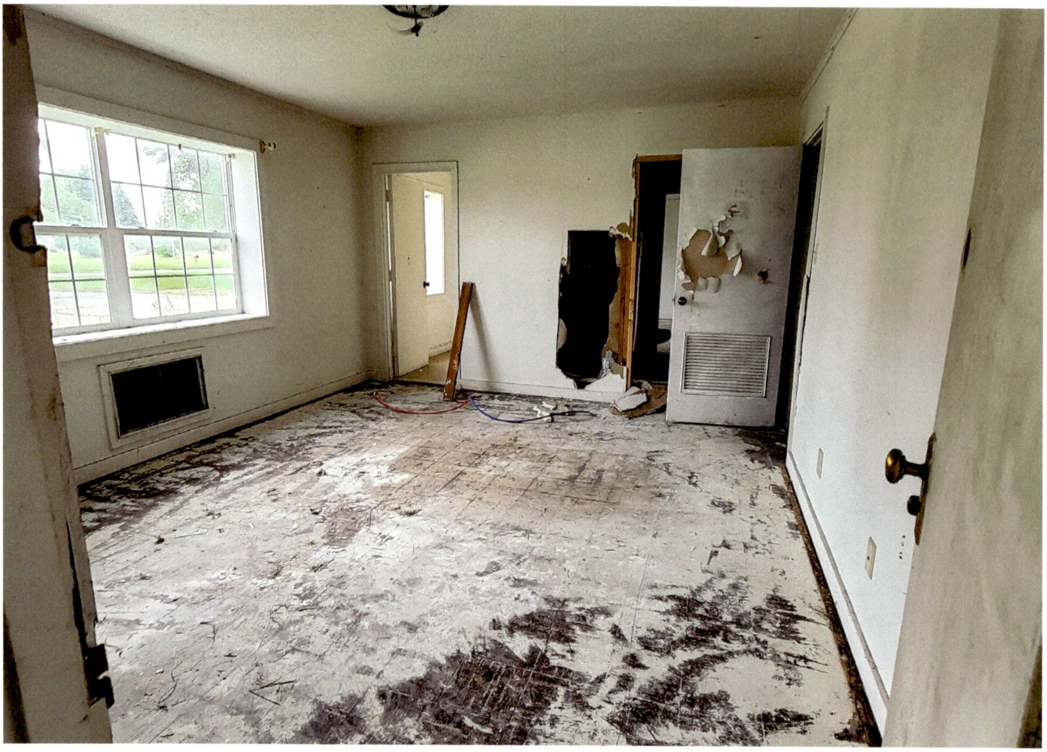

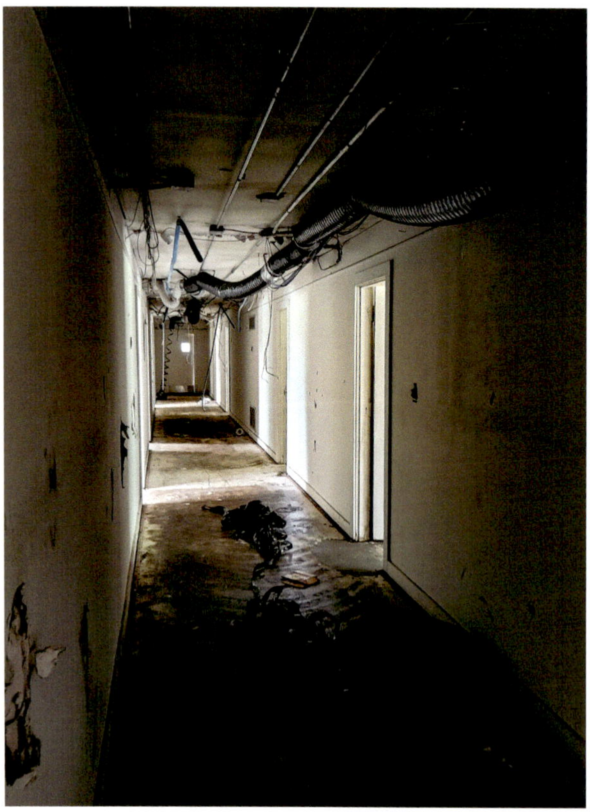

Above: Vandals had surprisingly made their way inside and started ripping out the pipes—not the best idea on a military base.

Left: I'm not sure why there were so many hose and chords hanging precariously from the ceiling in this hallway to other rooms.

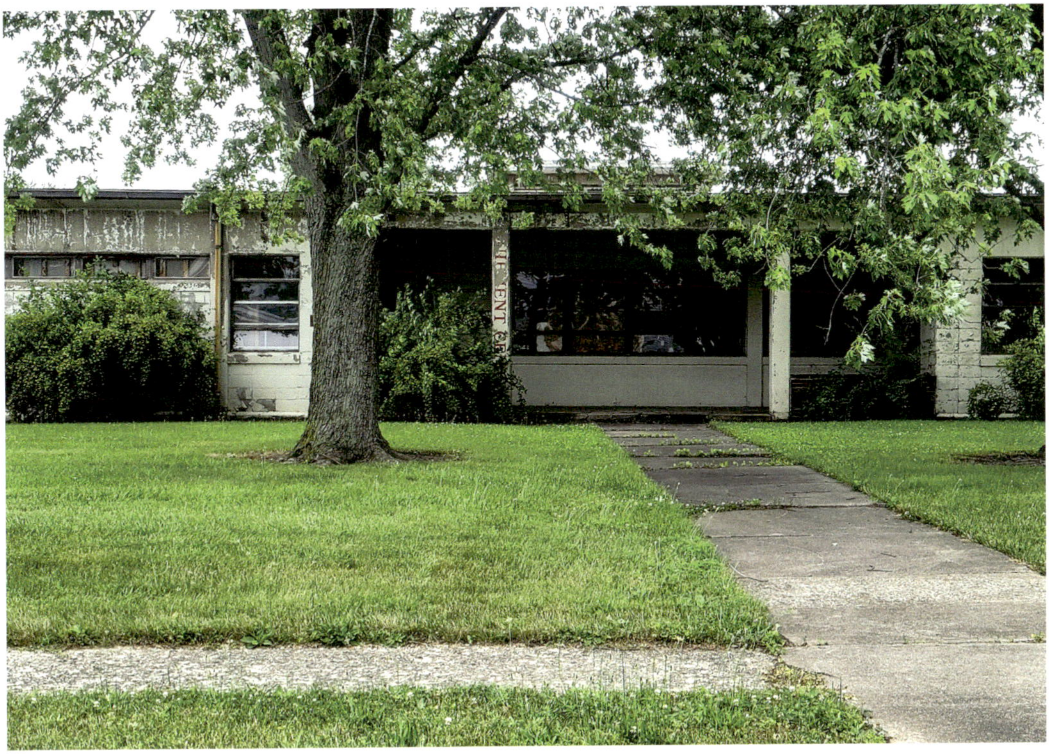

Above: One of the other disused buildings on the property.

Right: One of the twin Mark 33 3-inch/50-caliber gun mounts that dot the property. These would have been found on naval ships.

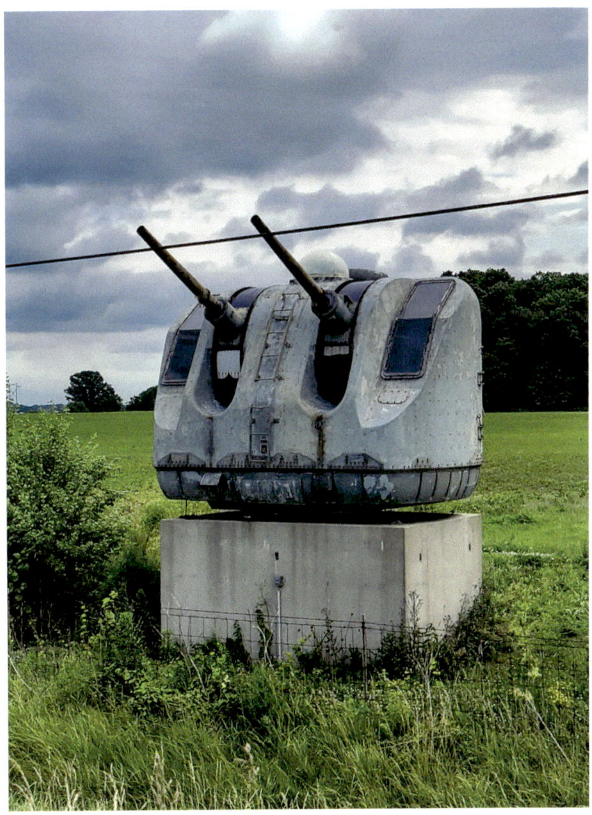

2

CROSSROADS OF AMERICA (US-40 & US-41)

The National Geographic Society stated in its November 1925 bulletin that "very nearly every vibrant city has to be a geographic crossroads before it can become a great city." The article listed some of the most spectacular crossroads in the globe, including the crossroads of the sea at the Panama Canal, the crossroads of cable lines in Guam, the crossroads of the air in Prague, and the crossroads of history in Palestine. Closer to home, though, "one of the most important individuals in the United States is the traffic policeman at the intersection of Washington and Meridian streets, Indianapolis. ... The Washington and Meridian streets intersection in Indianapolis is the crossroads of the principal transcontinental highways of the United States." The National Geographic Society's reference to Indianapolis in November 1925 wasn't the first or the last time an Indiana area would be referred to as the "Crossroads of America." The *Gary Post-Tribune* used the phrase to characterize Lake County earlier that year. At some point, Terre Haute was able to persuade the Indiana Historical Bureau that it was the real "Crossroads of America," as evidenced by a historical marker on the corner of Wabash Avenue and Seventh Street. Even earlier, in 1920, a Fort Wayne bank published an advertisement claiming that its home city was the crossroads. (Cierzniak)

The Indianapolis Chamber of Commerce formally endorsed "The Crossroads of America" as the city's motto in June 1926. In an effort to place additional signs bearing the motto on the city's outskirts, the chamber collaborated with the Hoosier Motor Club. The following year, the chamber began an innovative scheme in collaboration with local police that was described in the Chamber's newsletter in an effort to further the drive to establish itself as the "Crossroads of America": When the automobile with a foreign license approaches a traffic officer he immediately hails the motorist with a smile and a word of greeting, handing him a ticket which reads: "WELCOME TO INDIANAPOLIS! The Crossroads of America." (Cierzniak)

The majority of Indiana's roadways were built and maintained for the first sixty years of the state's existence by elected township officials or by private businesses who ran a system of toll roads. In the 1870s, counties were given the power to issue bonds to pay for the building and upkeep of highways. They were also given the power to buy the toll roads so that citizens could journey for free. However, because Indiana had not implemented any kind of standardized requirements, the condition of the roads at the turn of the century was continually inconsistent. To make matters worse, a dated legislation that allowed farmers and other able-bodied men to "work out" their taxes as inexperienced road hands resulted in millions of dollars being wasted annually on substandard construction. According to a representative of the U.S. Department of Agriculture, "the work of road building in Indiana is in the control of men who know less about road construction than they know about astronomy," as stated in *The Indianapolis Star* in February 1909. State highway commissions were set up in thirty-five states by 1910 in order to supervise road building and maintenance and impose consistent standards. Before the General Assembly passed legislation creating the Indiana Highway Commission, another seven years would pass. Indianapolis was among the first cities in Indiana to mark the beginning of the "good roads" period. The city celebrated the completion of the first paved section of the National Old Trails (U.S. 40) east from the city boundaries to the Hancock County boundary in September 1917 with a ribbon-cutting ceremony and parade. The size of the state highway system would more than triple in a short period of time, and gravel would be replaced by hard-surface paving on the majority of key thoroughfares. A universal numbering system would be implemented, in order to assist the increasing number of out-of-state drivers using Indiana's highways, along with the first gas tax, which would be levied at a rate of two cents per gallon. The Indiana General Assembly passed House Concurrent Resolution 6 on March 2, 1937, designating "The Crossroads of America" as the state's official "motto or slogan." Carthage (Missouri), Effingham (Illinois), and Vandalia (Ohio), which even featured a "Crossroads of America" motel, were among the other cities to claim the moniker "Crossroads of America" about the same period. But even as rivals for the prized designation appeared from every angle, Indiana quickly found itself trying to hold onto its renown as a crossroads.

Indiana's bridges are collapsing, the road surface is deteriorating, and Indiana is lagging behind neighboring states in spending for roadways. According to a 1948 report by the State Highway Commission, these issues still resonate today.

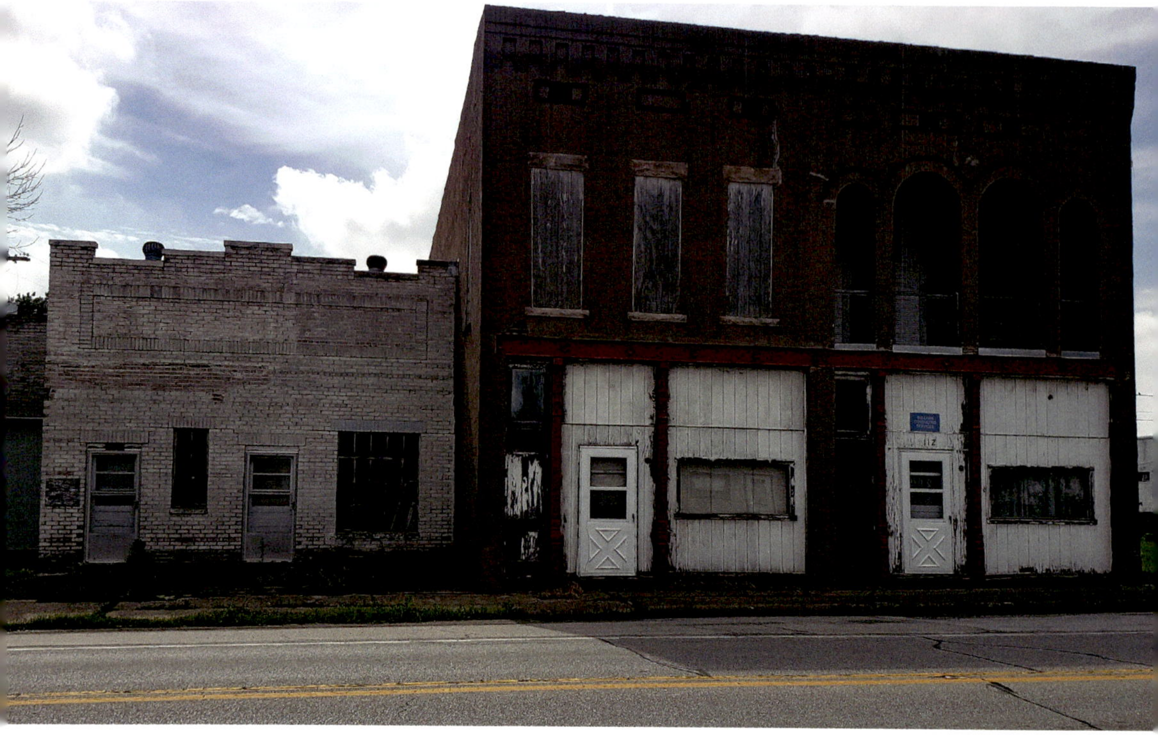

Shuttered businesses on a main street in one of the many small towns bypassed by the highway.

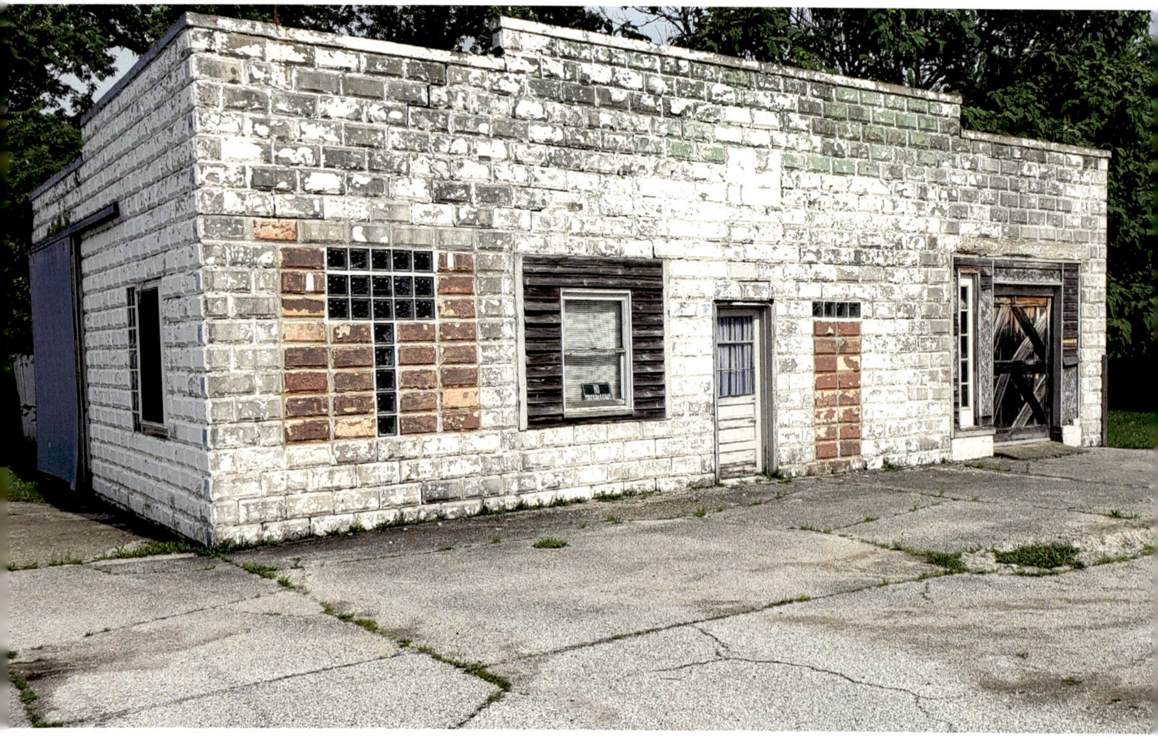

Another closed business along the main drag. The brickwork on this one was outstanding.

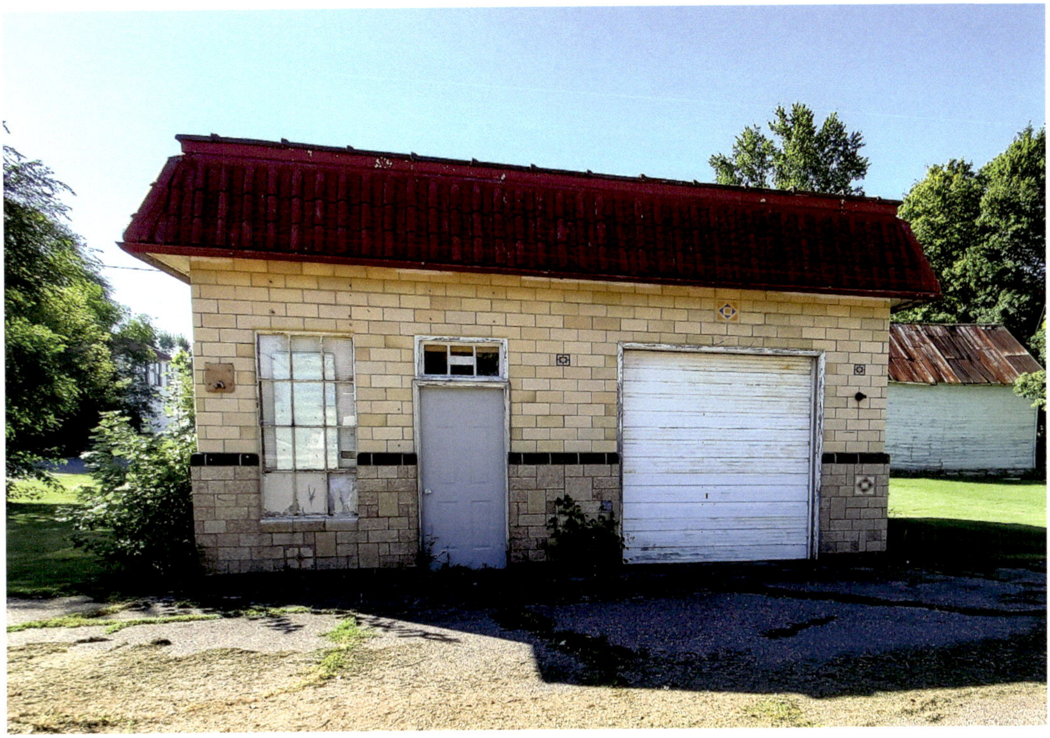

The remains of a small garage that closed ten years prior.

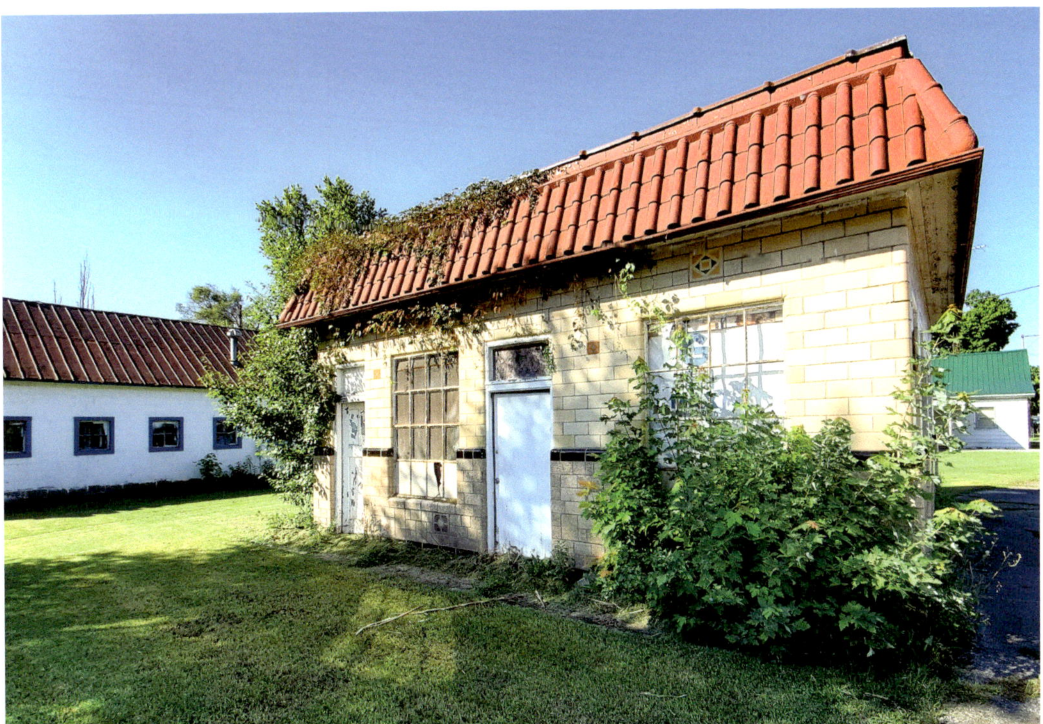

The sidewalk that led to the office and bathroom has become overgrown to the point you can barely distinguish it.

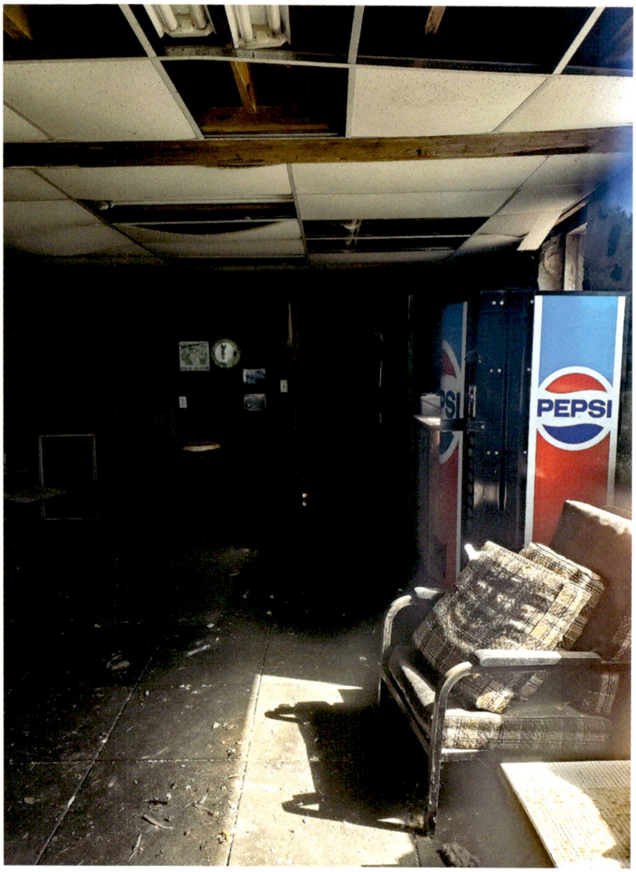

Left: Peering inside the waiting room, there's still a Pepsi vending machine and what looks to be a very comfortable chair left behind.

Below: I was surprised that the windows of this closed convenience store were covered. We were unable to find a way to see inside.

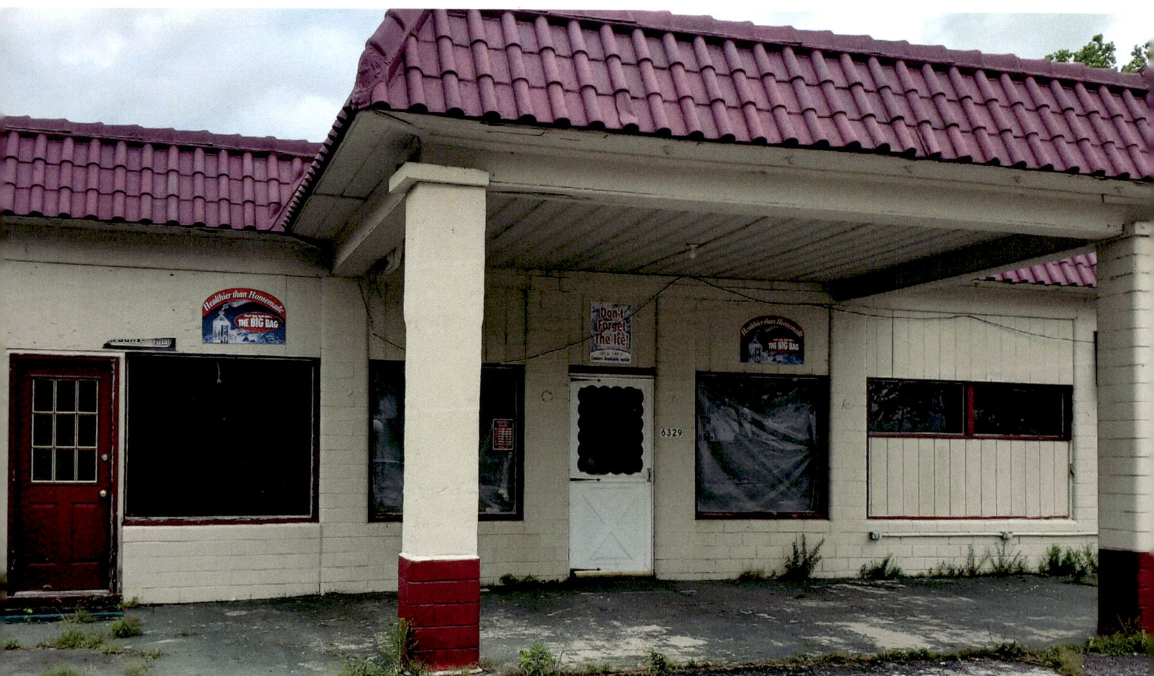

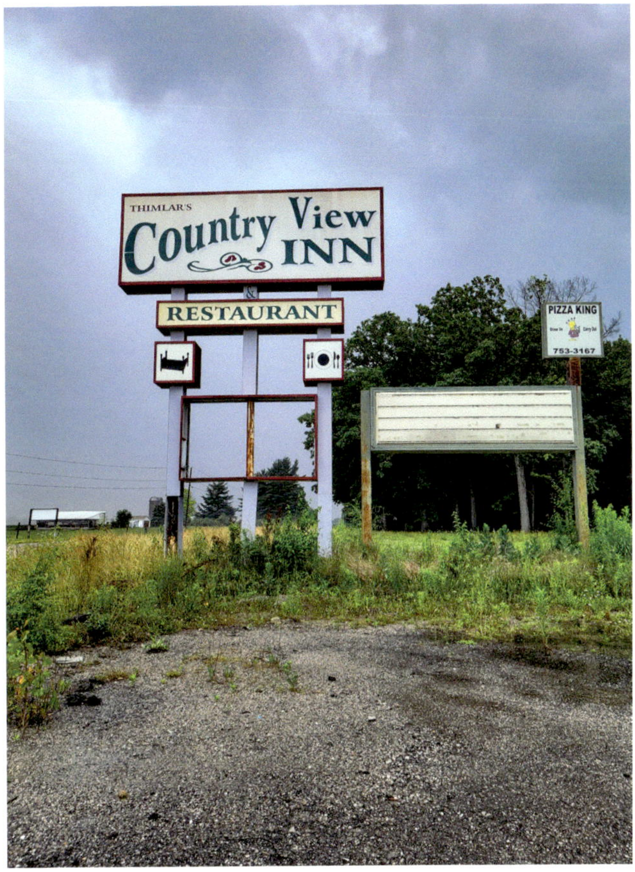

Right: A sign alerting those on the state road that there was a place to sleep and a hot meal available.

Below: The only building that remained on the property after a 2018 fire tore through the hotel and Pizza King.

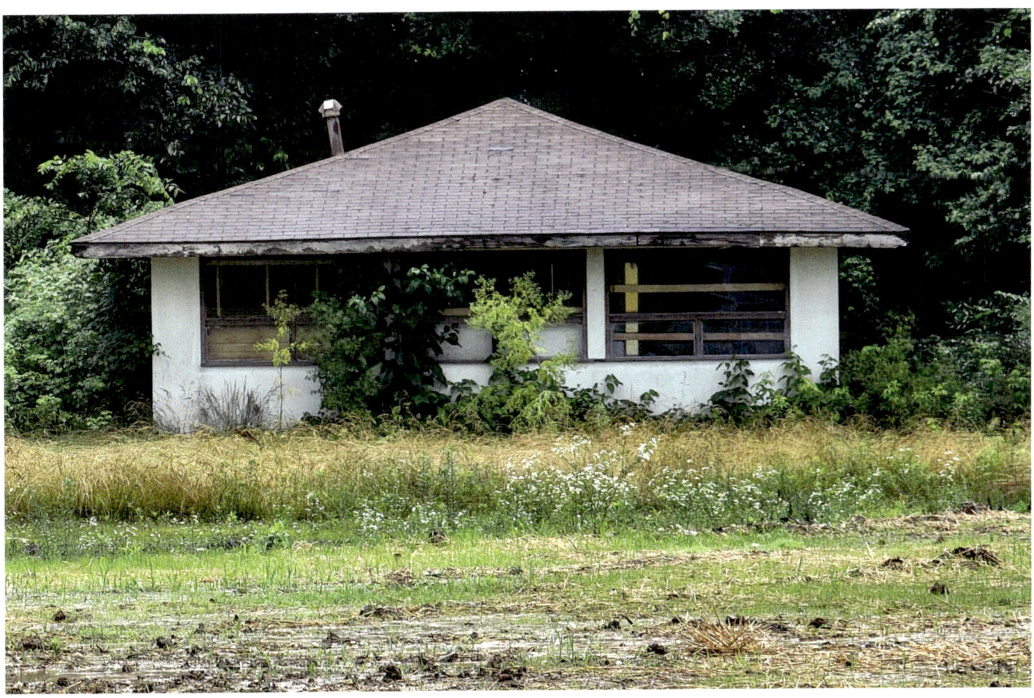

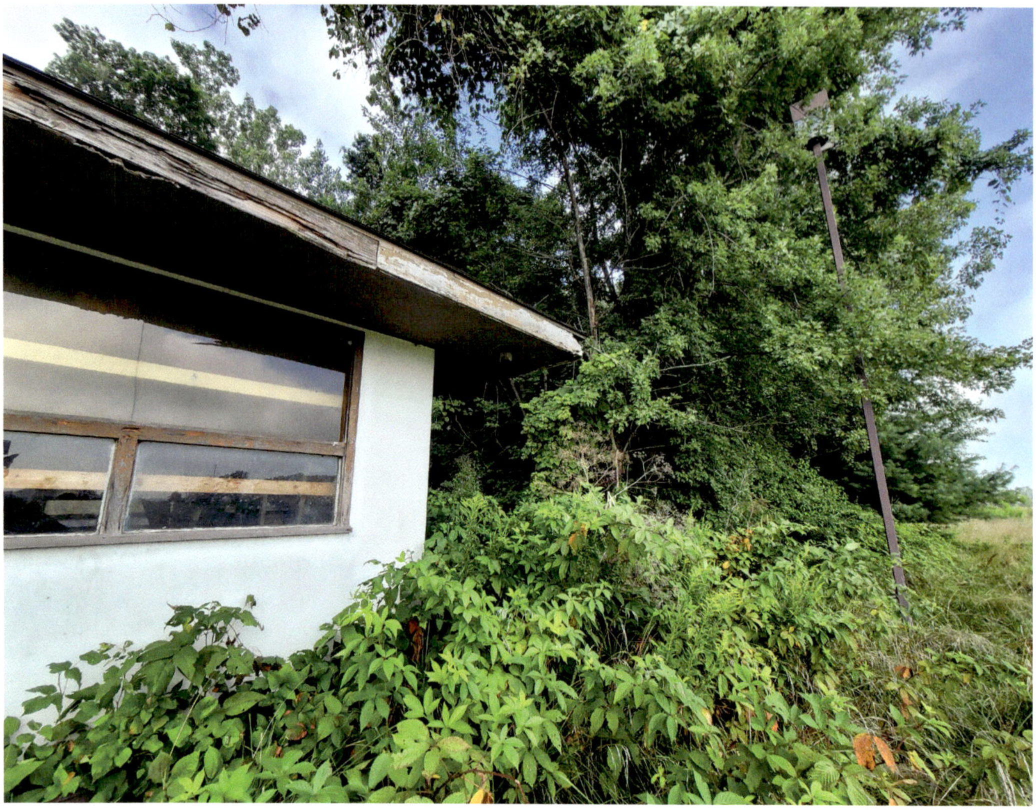

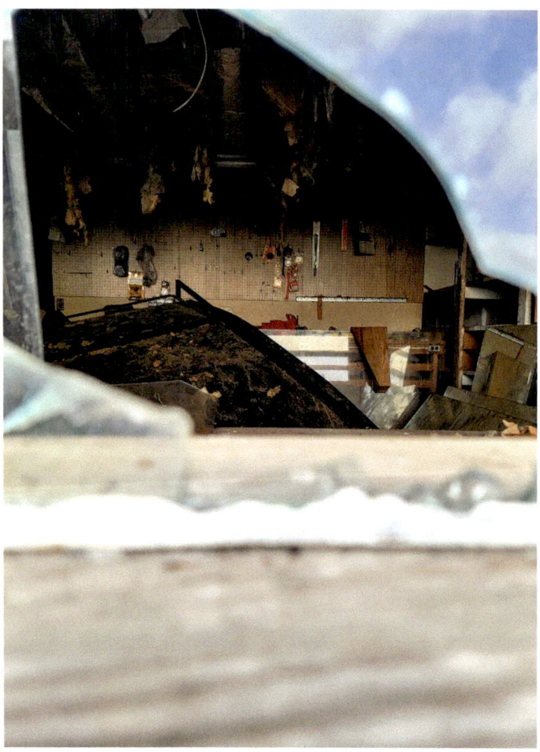

Above: The last building has started to become overgrown and hidden, much like the parking lot lights.

Left: A look inside the last building, which looks to be a maintenance shed/building for the property.

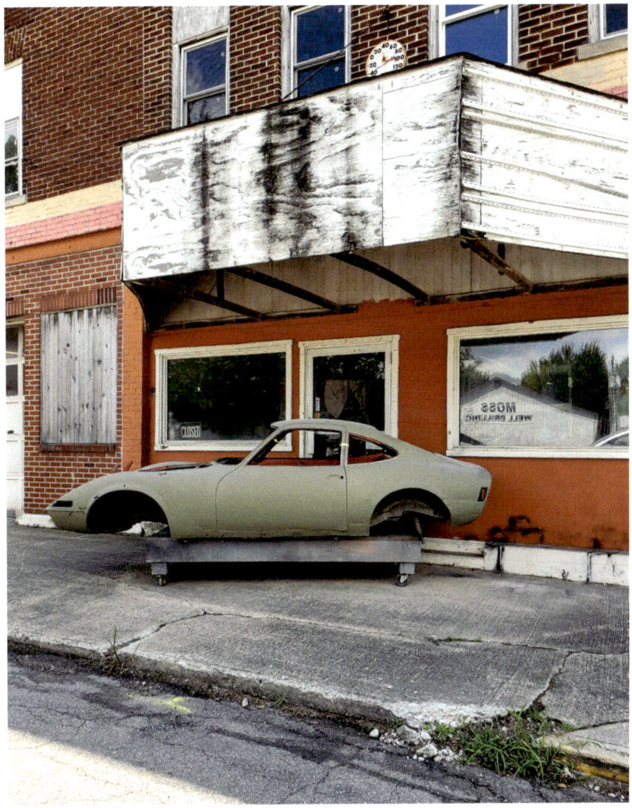

An Opel GT sits outside a defunct movie theater on a main street.

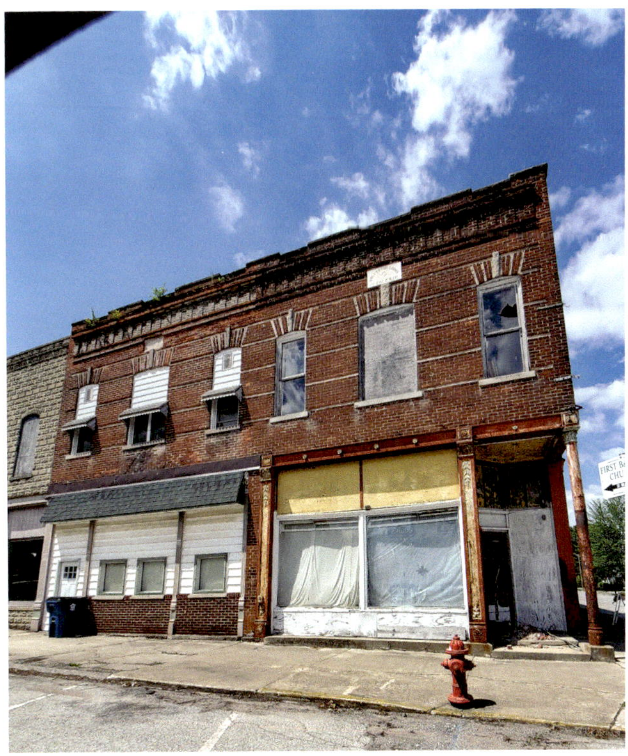

The former Galveston Lodge that now sits empty, with plants growing in the gutters and on the roof.

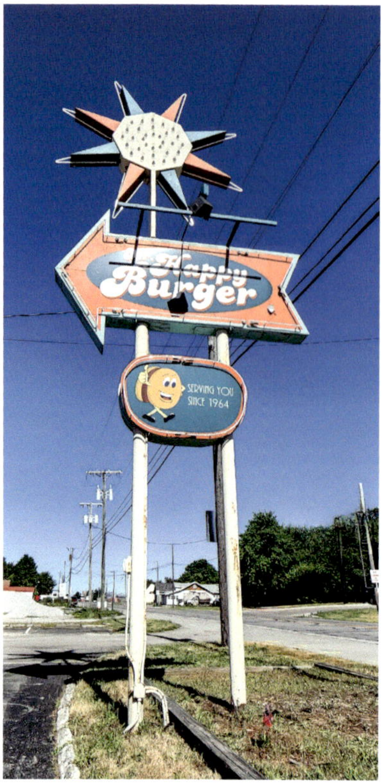

Left: A vintage style sign for a defunct restaurant off a main street.

Below: At one point, the restaurant would have been a drive-in and used primarily in the warm months. At some point it became a drive-through/eat-in before becoming disused.

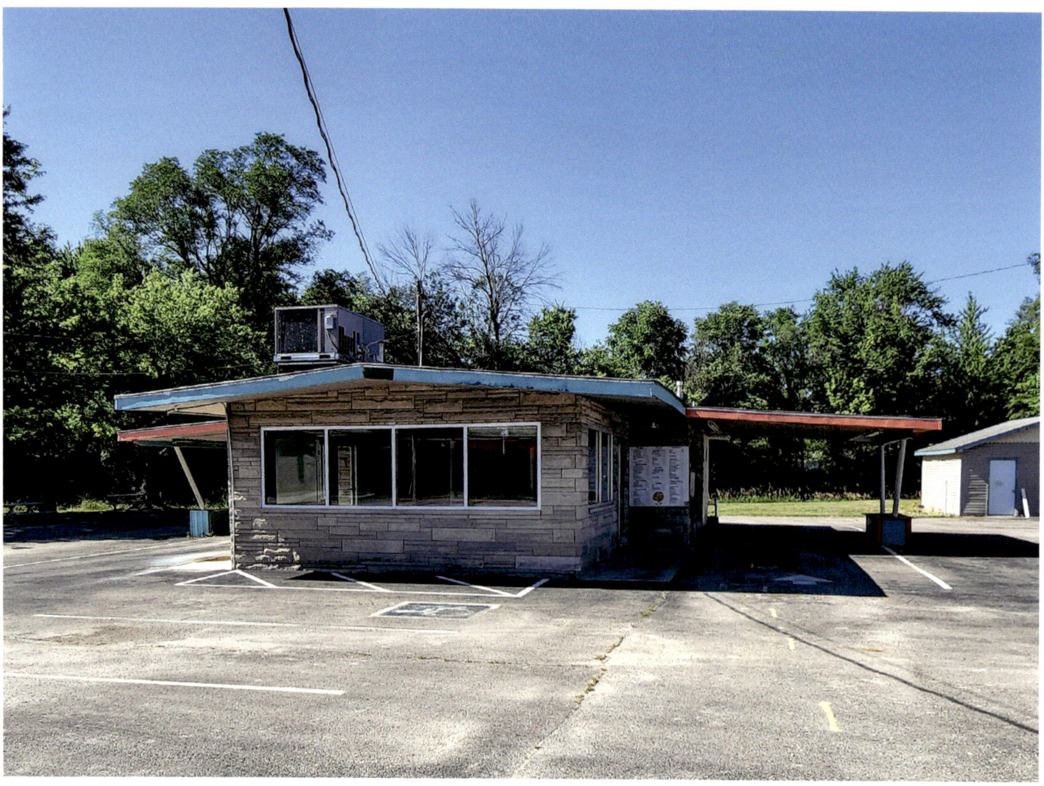

Right: One of Indiana's remaining Carnegie libraries.

Below: A total of 2,509 Carnegie libraries were built between 1883 and 1929.

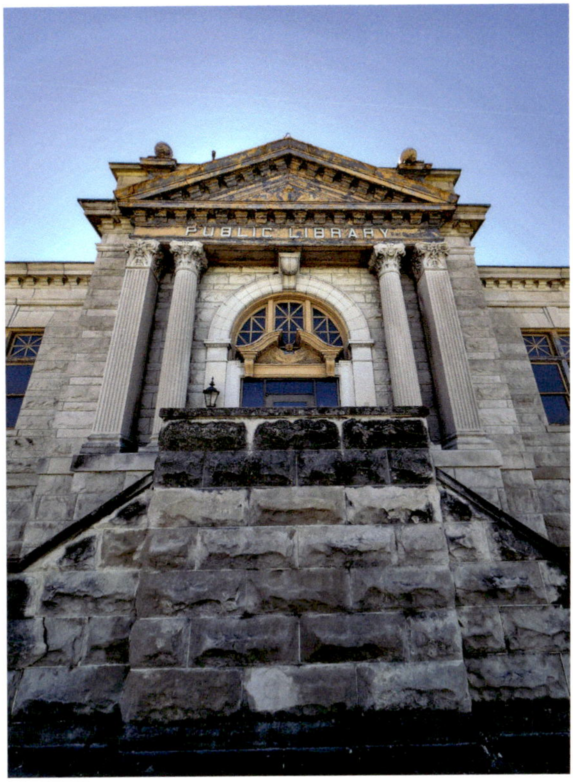

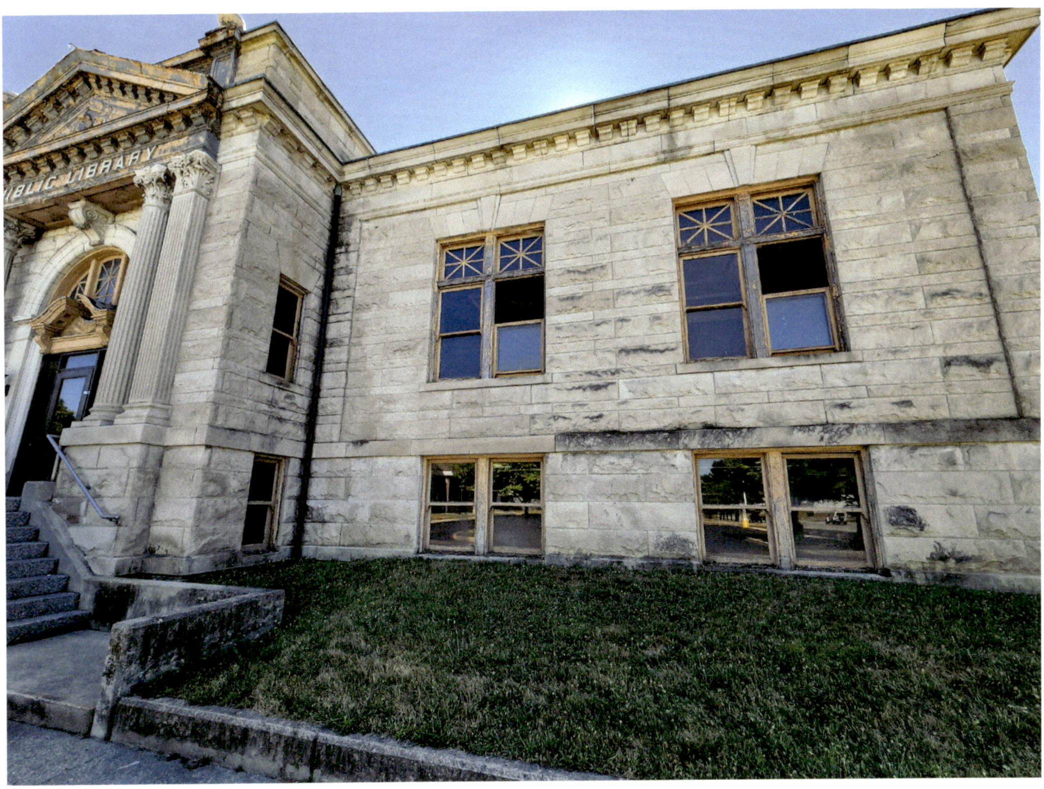

3

THE INTERSTATE SYSTEM AND THE DEATH OF SMALL COMMUNITIES

Automobiles sped right into the heart of Hoosiers' lives in the years following World War II. The auto factories in Indiana were operating nonstop in an effort to meet the postwar demand. The United Auto Workers (UAW) union obtained better pay, improved pension plans, and health care for its members as the Big Three's (General Motors, Chrysler, and Ford) earnings soared. While Indiana's postwar economy was being fueled by the production of cars, the product itself was altering the environment and how Hoosiers lived. (Madison and Sandweiss)

The Federal Aid Highway Act was approved by President Dwight D. Eisenhower in 1956. The "Dwight D. Eisenhower National System of Interstate and Defense Highways" was established pursuant to this bill. The main clause of the law stated that controlled access roads would be used to build the "interstates," which would connect important locations across the country and be paid for with 90% federal funds, as opposed to the 50/50 split that had previously been used to fund road upgrades. The Act of 1956, along with laws enacted in 1916 and 1921, was the third such Federal Aid road law to be passed up to that point. Many people thought that after the bill was approved, the money would be used to upgrade and/or construct the most crucial highways in each state. In 1944, the concept of an "interstate highway system" was established. To support the war effort, this system relied heavily on U.S. Highways to transport soldiers and supplies across the nation. This was the concept that set the Eisenhower Administration on the path to developing the modern interstate system.

Before there were super freeways, a small town's only hope for survival were historic roadways. As they moved through the town, each made a turn onto the "Main Street." Towns had previously sprouted up all over the country along the train lines that connected the country's coasts. The prosperous farms and peaceful meadows that brought Indiana prosperity now give way to historic villages with traditional main streets and lush residential neighborhoods. The buildings and landscapes that previous generations have left behind allow you to literally trace the nation's westward migration, from the Federal-style architecture of an early pike town (a town that offered traveling accommodations but little else) to the drive-ins and stainless-steel diners of the 1940s. The Historic National Road is a tranquil drive thanks to the byway's small-town antique shops and vintage fueling stations. The environment is dominated by expansive views of far-off farms and barns, as well as grazing livestock. In other places, approaching communities are signaled by water towers, church steeples, and courthouse towers, which attract you from the vast spaces into the old towns. The topography of the terrain allows for glances into natural regions that are largely concealed in the rural landscape as well as views down the corridor. (Arnold) Taking the route less traveled has always served us well and is how we find the interesting parts of Indiana.

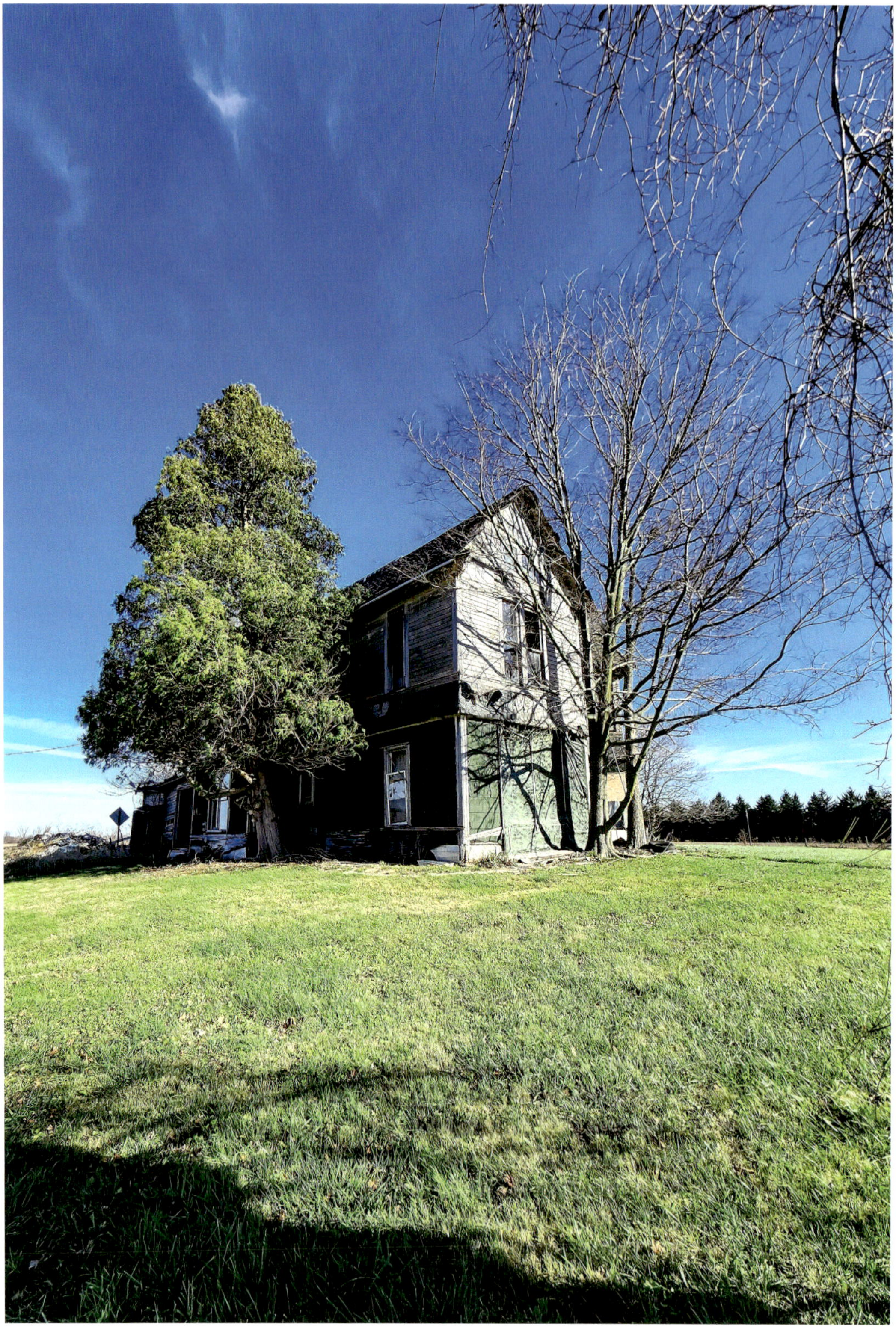

This was a location I found based on some vague directions from someone else's photos.

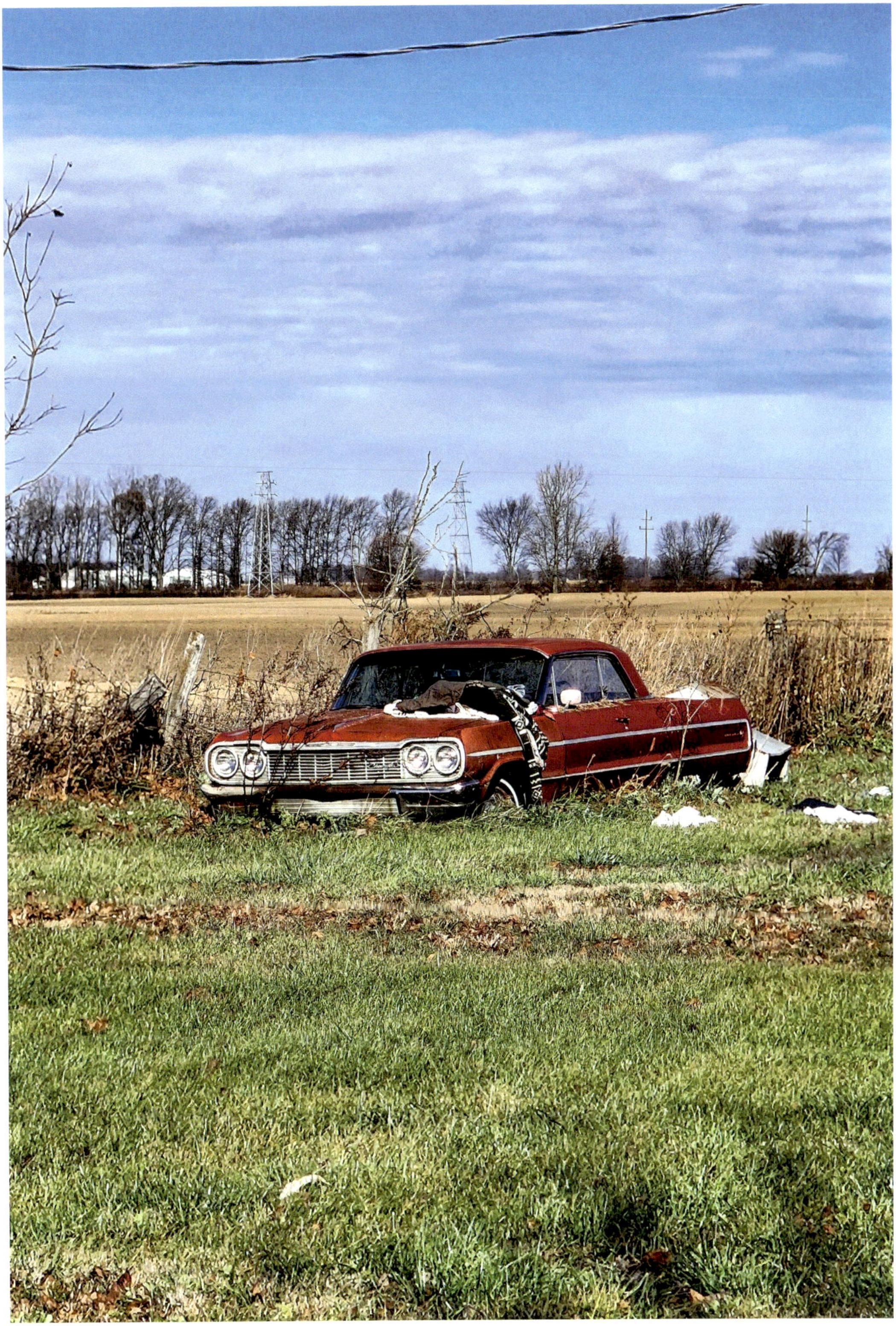

A chevy Impala sitting on the edge of the corn field with multiple jackets and sweaters sitting on the hood.

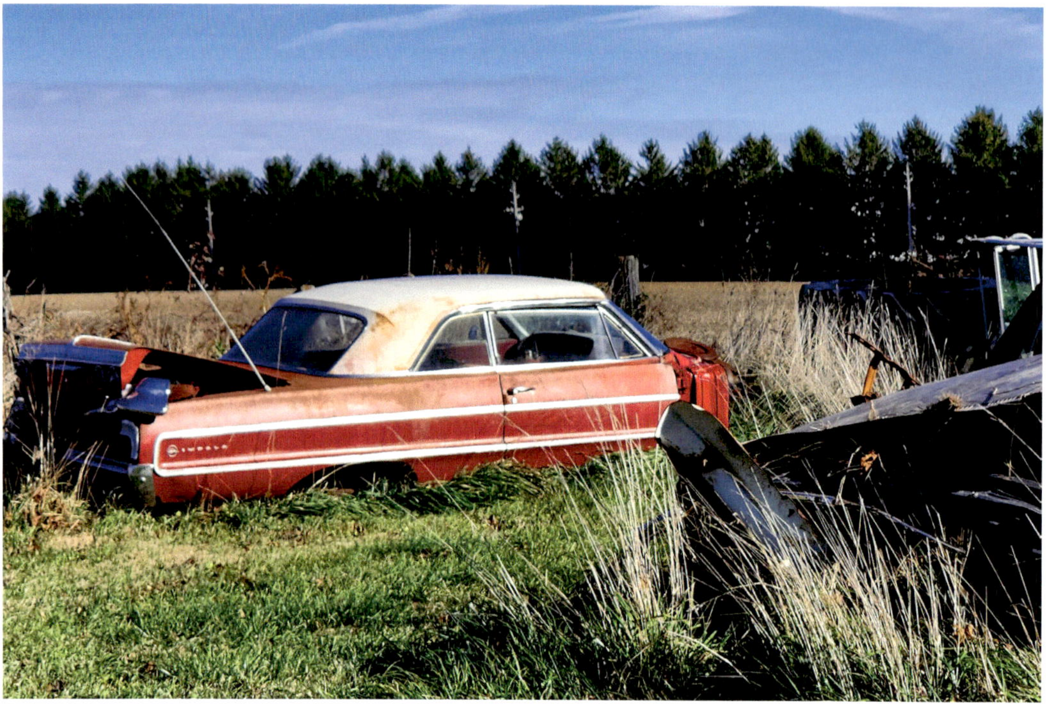

A second Chevy Impala, this one without an engine or front end, sits on the back edge of the property.

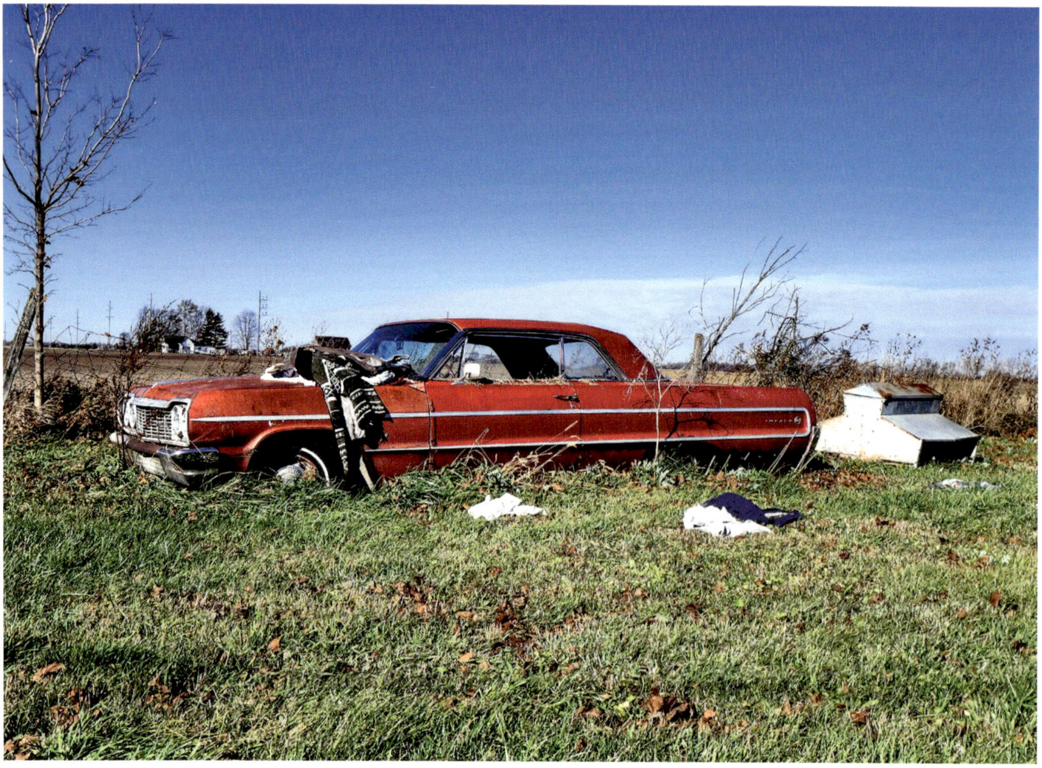

A better shot of the intact Chevy Impala and the miscellaneous clothing remains that surround it.

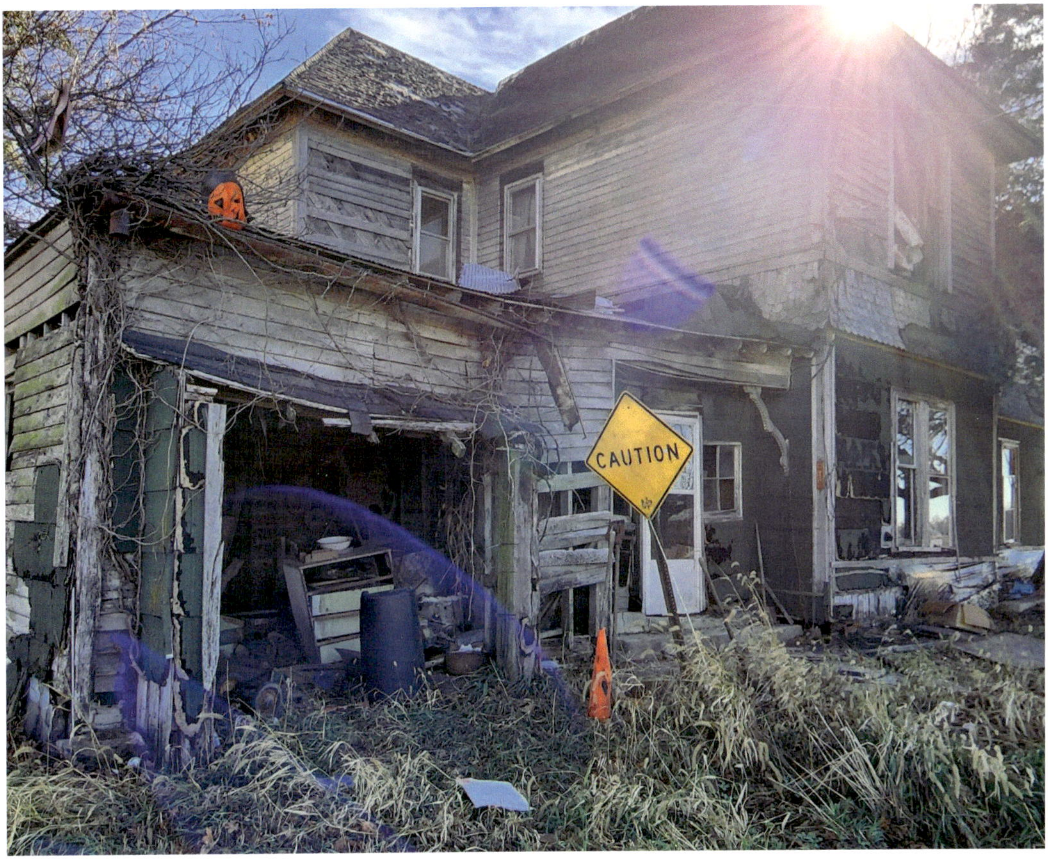

Above: This house had a caution sign leading into its garage, which, considering the state of the property, was relevant.

Right: A nonworking promotional thermometer from the local power company still hangs outside the garage.

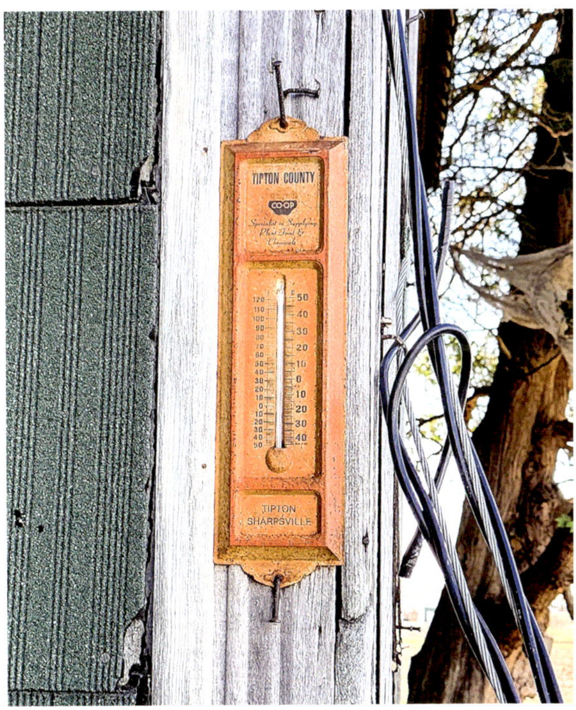

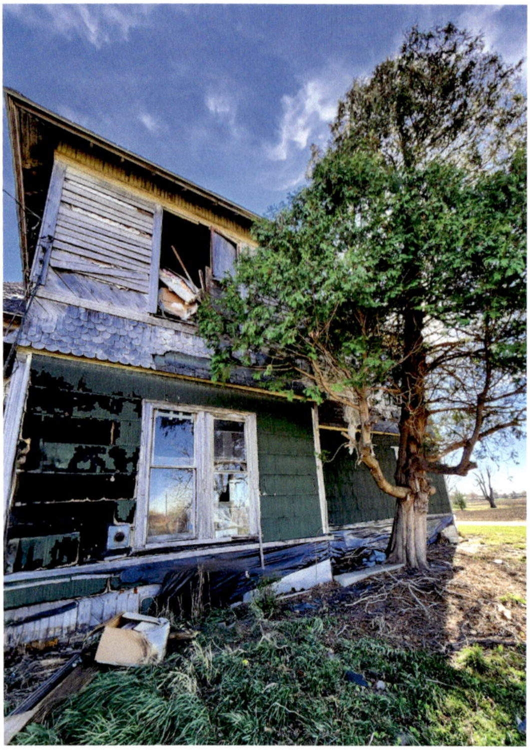

Left: The top floor had substantial damage from the summer storms, and much of what was in that bedroom littered the lawn.

Below: The front of the house as seen from the street.

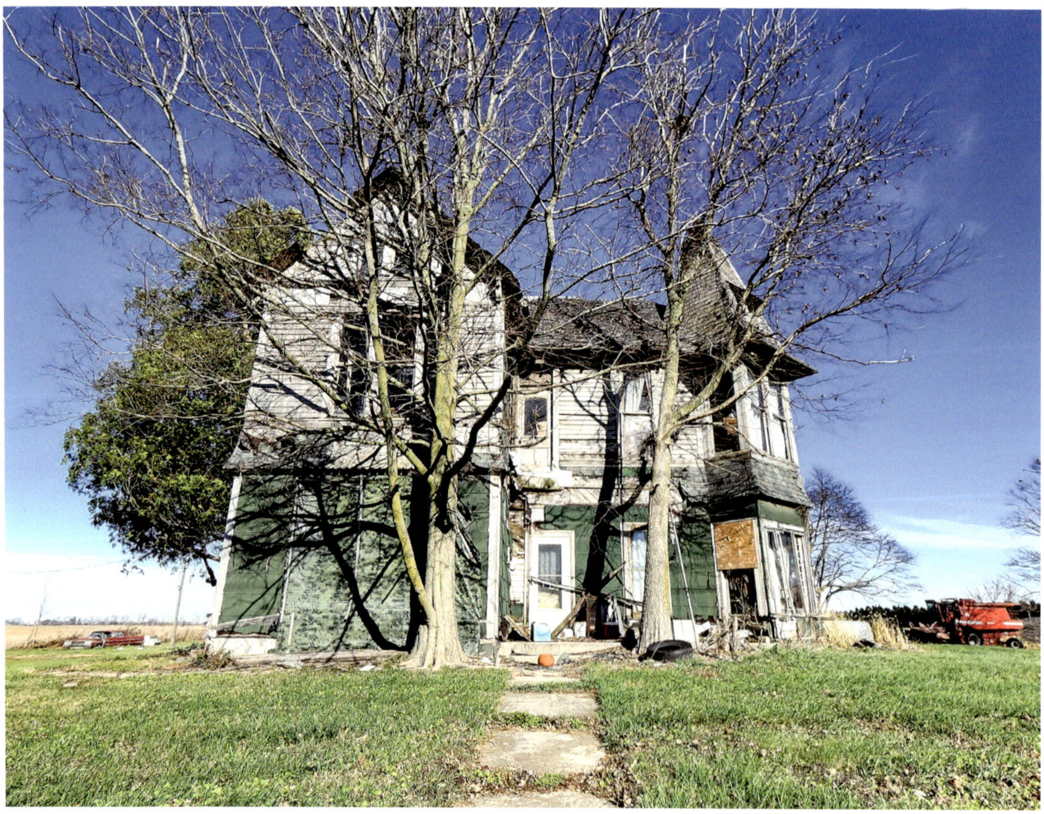

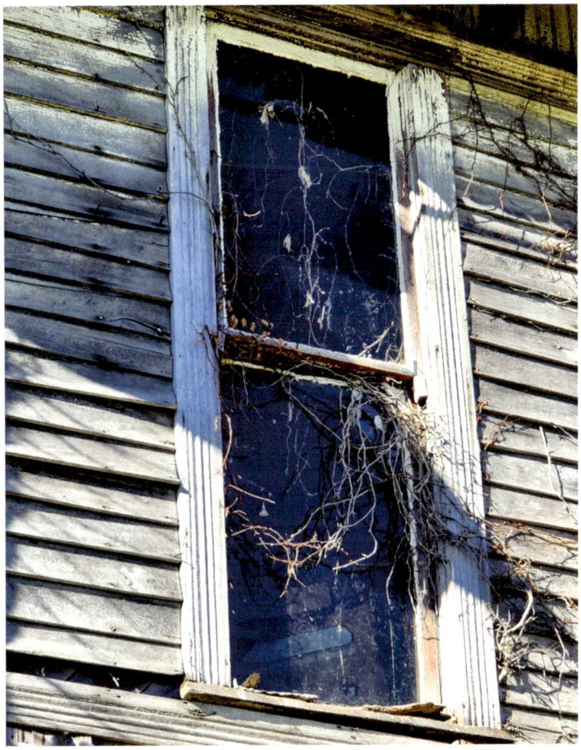

Nature has slowly started reclaiming the house.

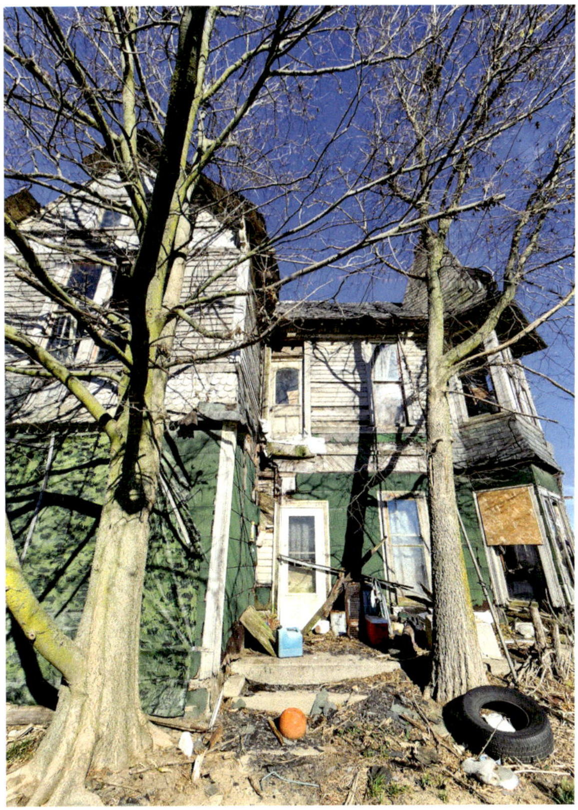

At one point there was an upstairs balcony as evidenced from the upstairs door to nowhere.

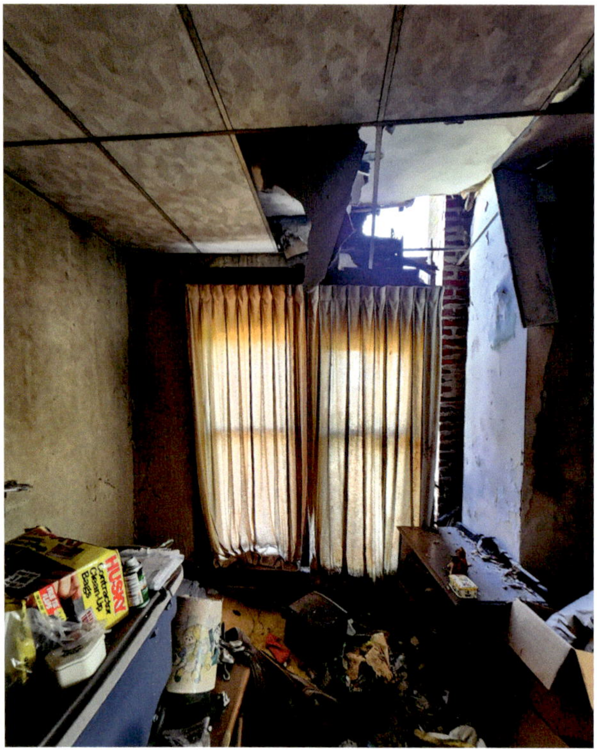

Inside the dining room, the ceiling and wall above the window have started to crumble, letting in copious amounts of sunlight.

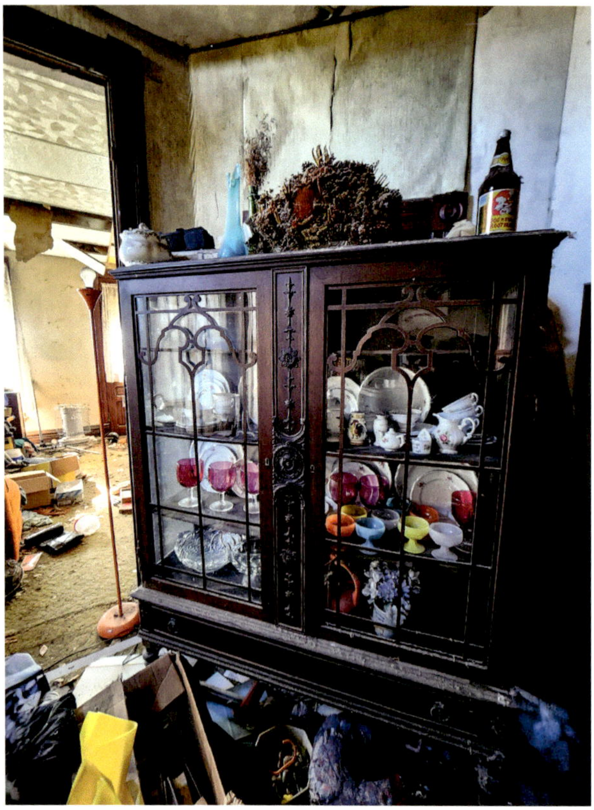

A locked china cabinet, which has pieces of uranium glass on display.

Right: The living room had absolutely beautiful stained glass surrounding the front windows. It was impossible for us to go further inside due to the state of the flooring.

Below: Farmhouse that we came across on one of the state roads.

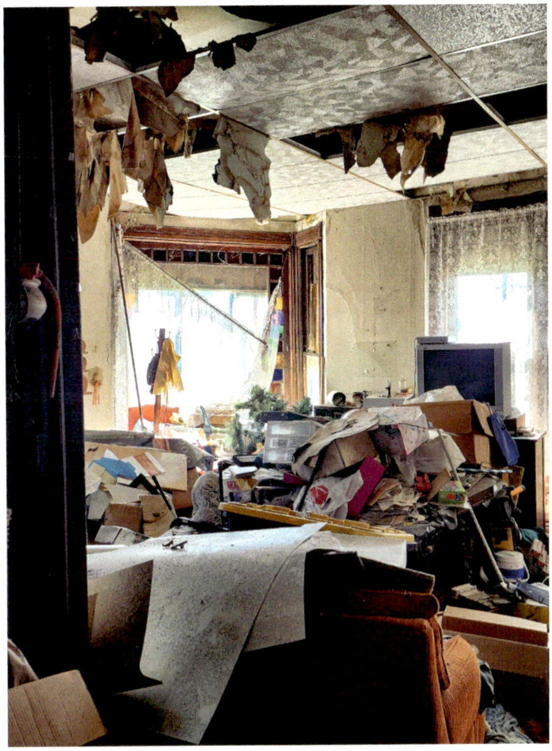

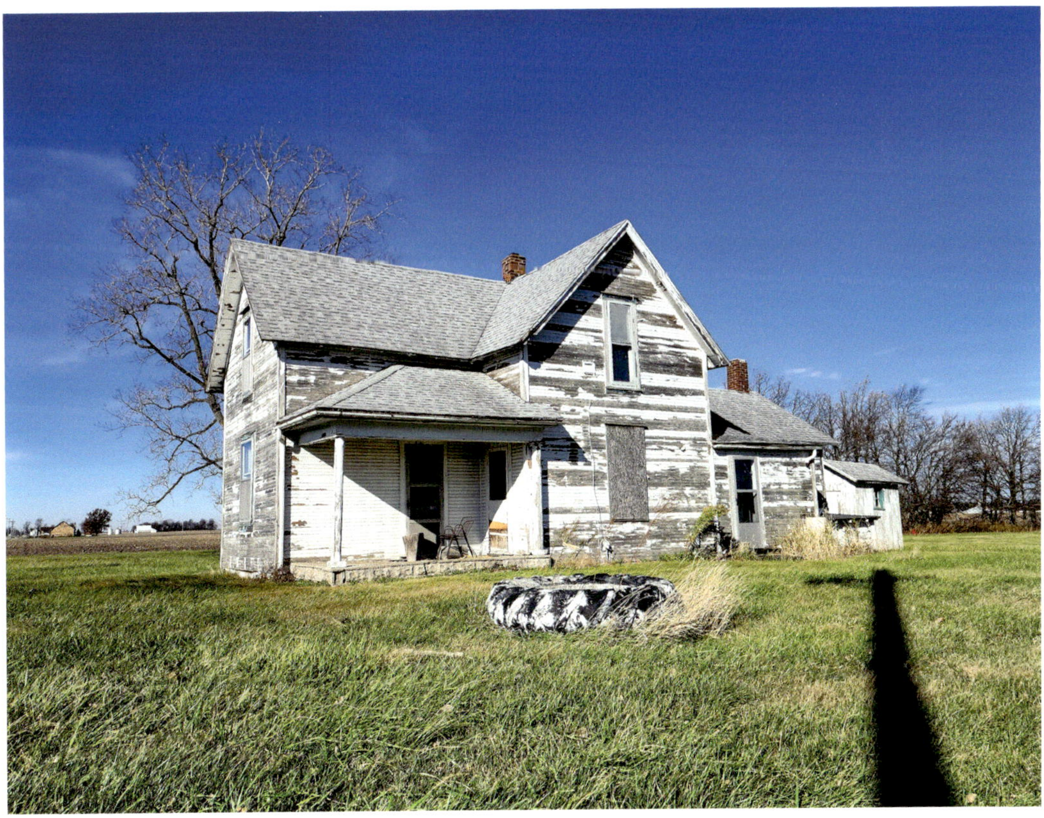

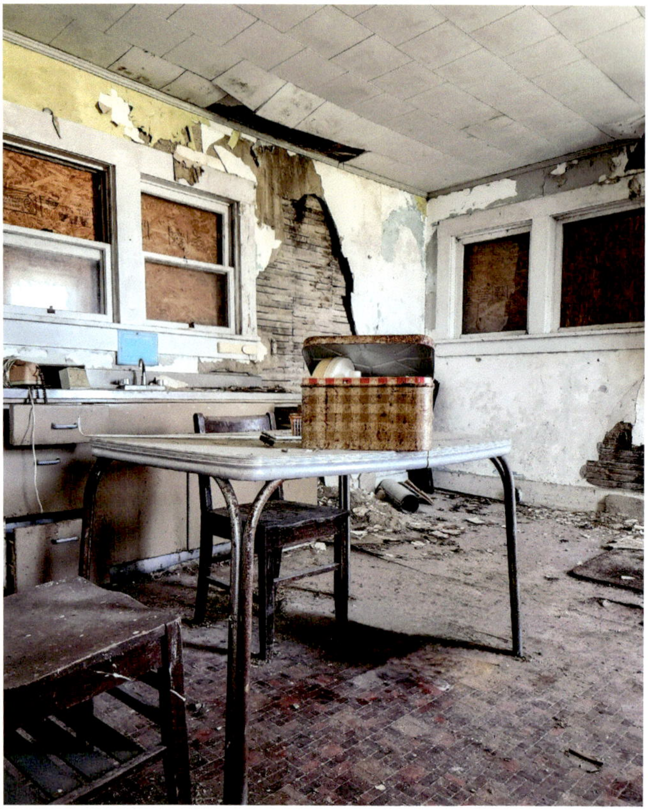

Left: Most of the kitchen was color schemed in a light beige/pink, which also included a phone left on the counter.

Below: A picnic basket was still neatly packed and waiting on the kitchen table.

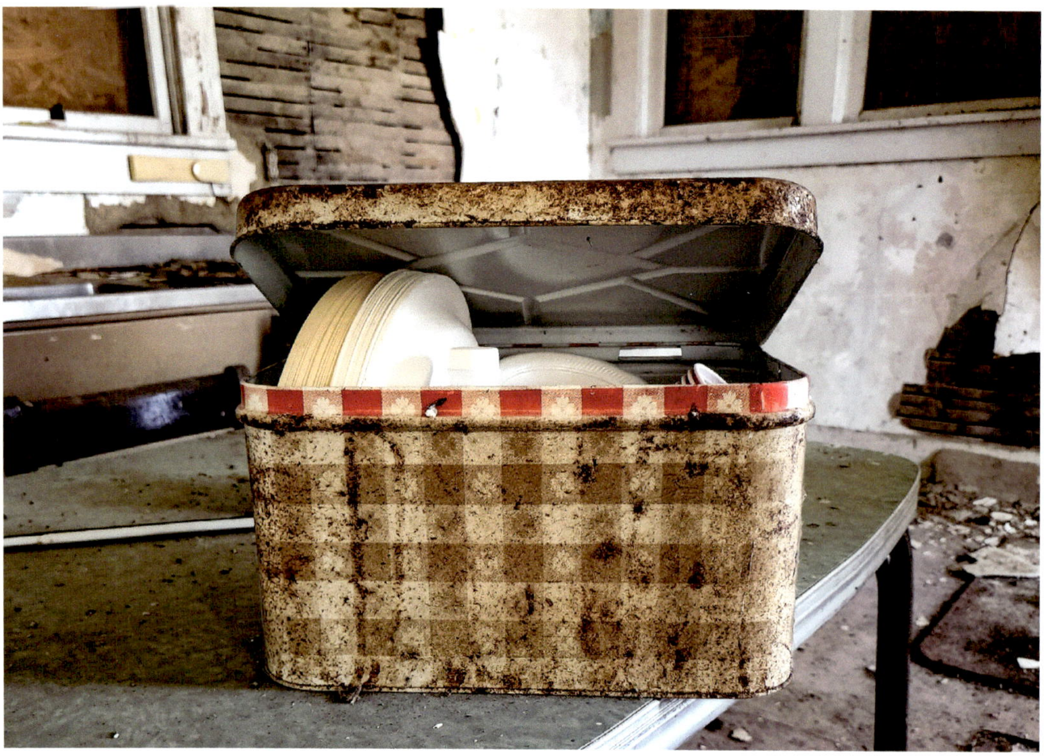

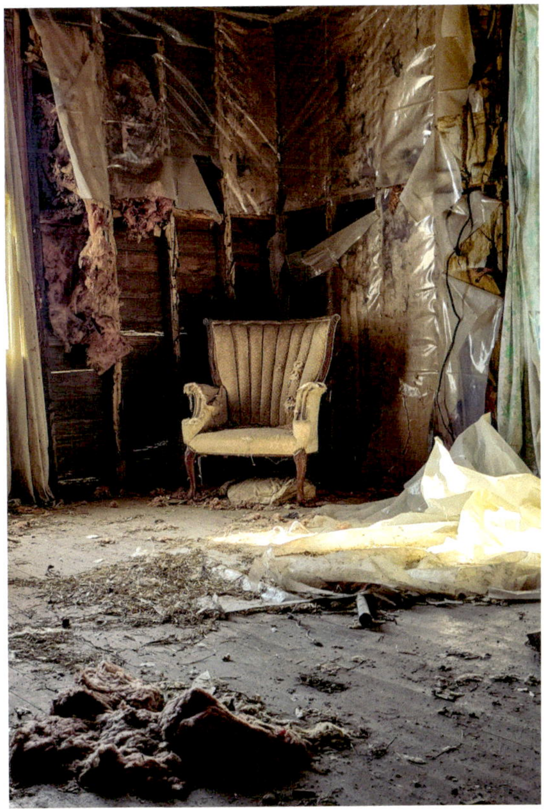

Right: A vintage wingback chair sits in the corner of the remains of the living room.

Below: Two chairs sit separated by a glass coffee table in the remains of the living room.

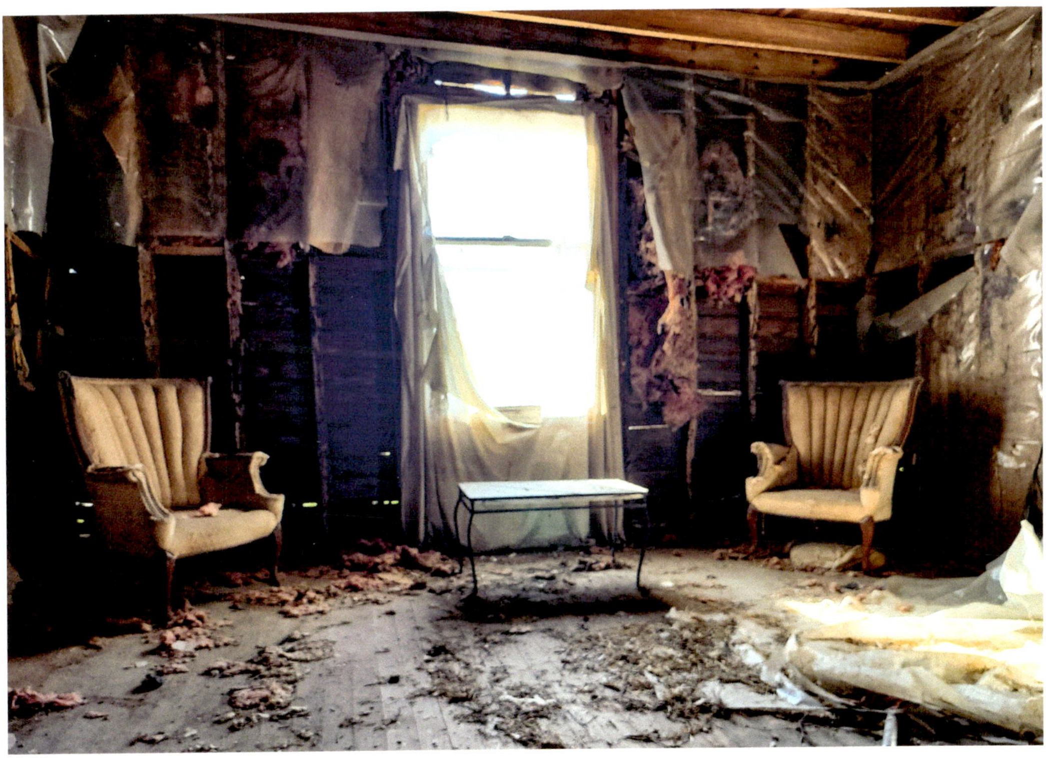

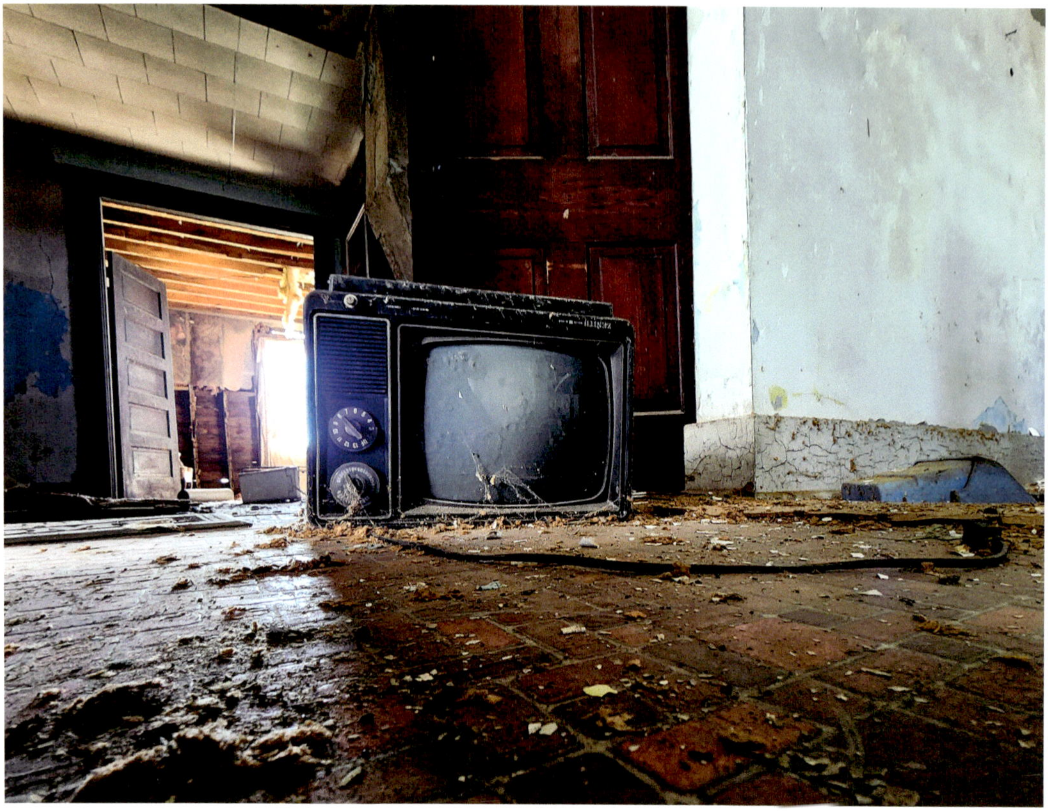

There was a small television left on the floor. Televisions are my absolute favorite thing to find.

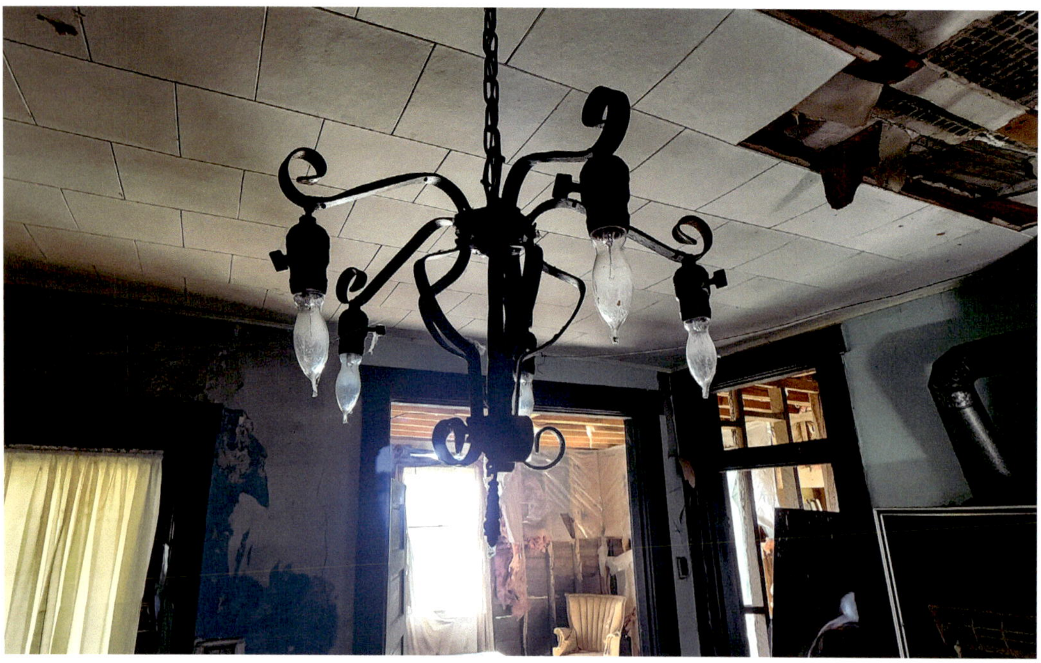

This light fixture was gorgeous.

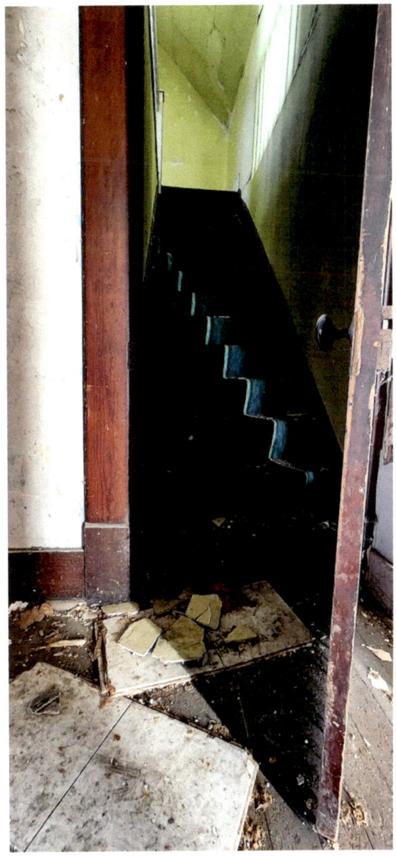

Righ: The stairs led to a very unremarkable upstairs.

Below: This house was up a fairly steep hill that we hiked on one of the coldest days of the year.

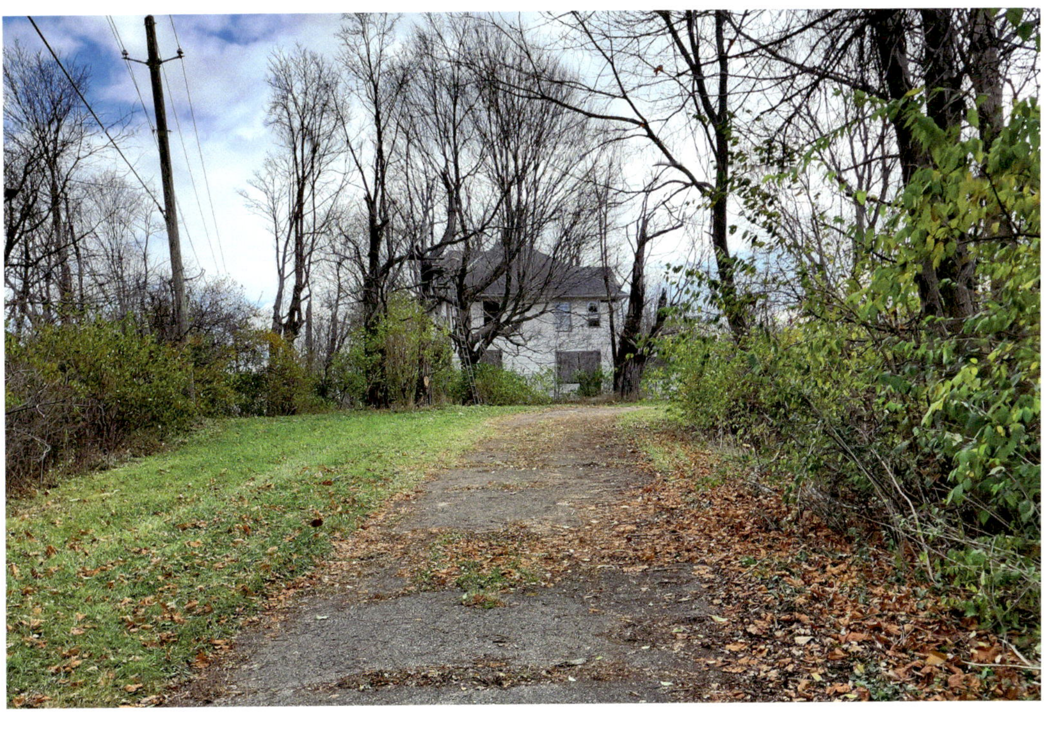

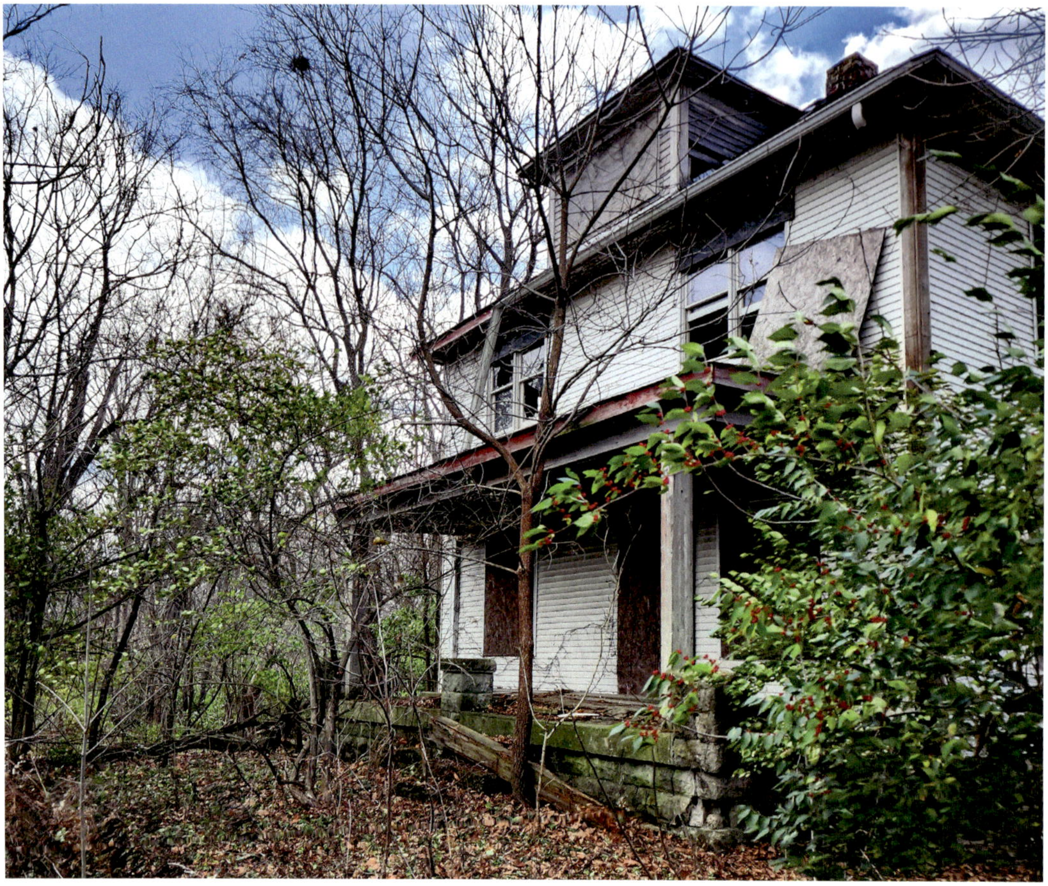

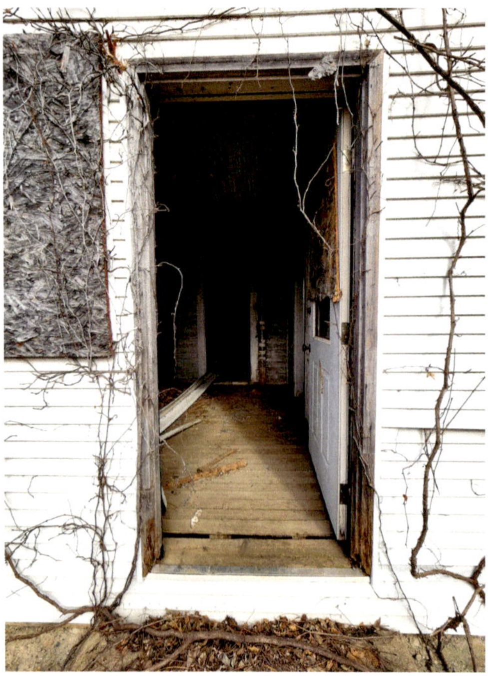

Above: You could only see the roof from the road.

Left: The back door was left wide open, which is how we found our way inside.

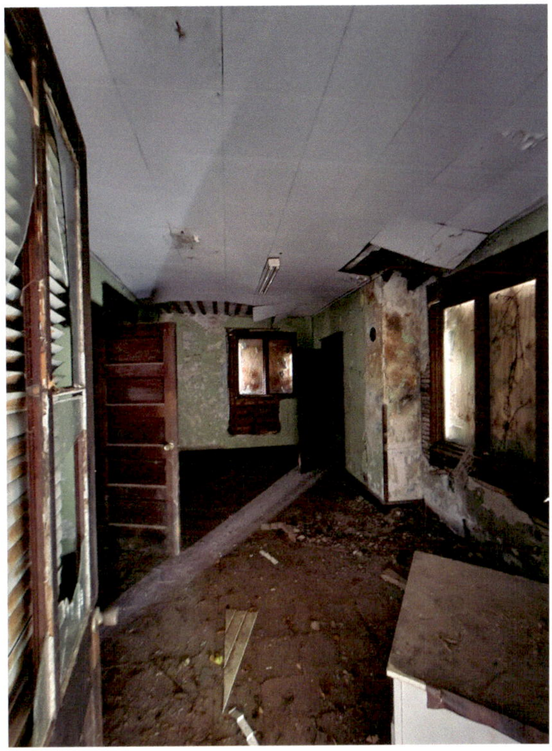

Right: The first room upon entering the house was the kitchen.

Below: The former living room with a couch and television left behind.

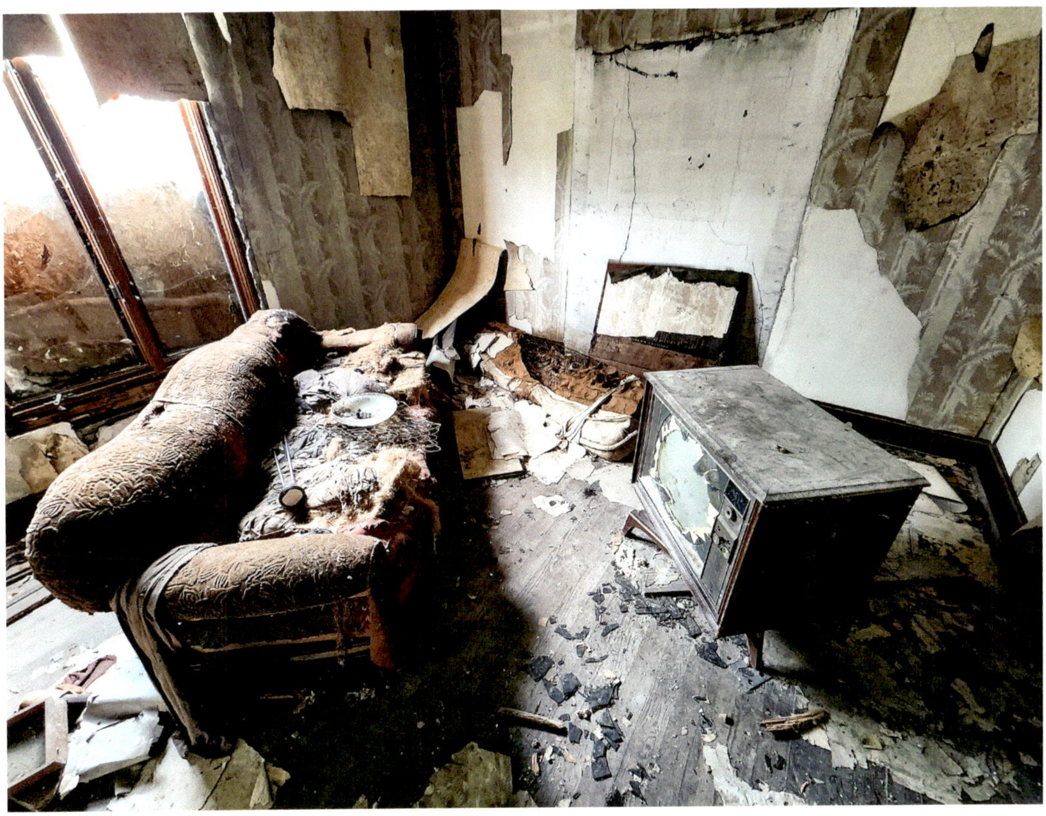

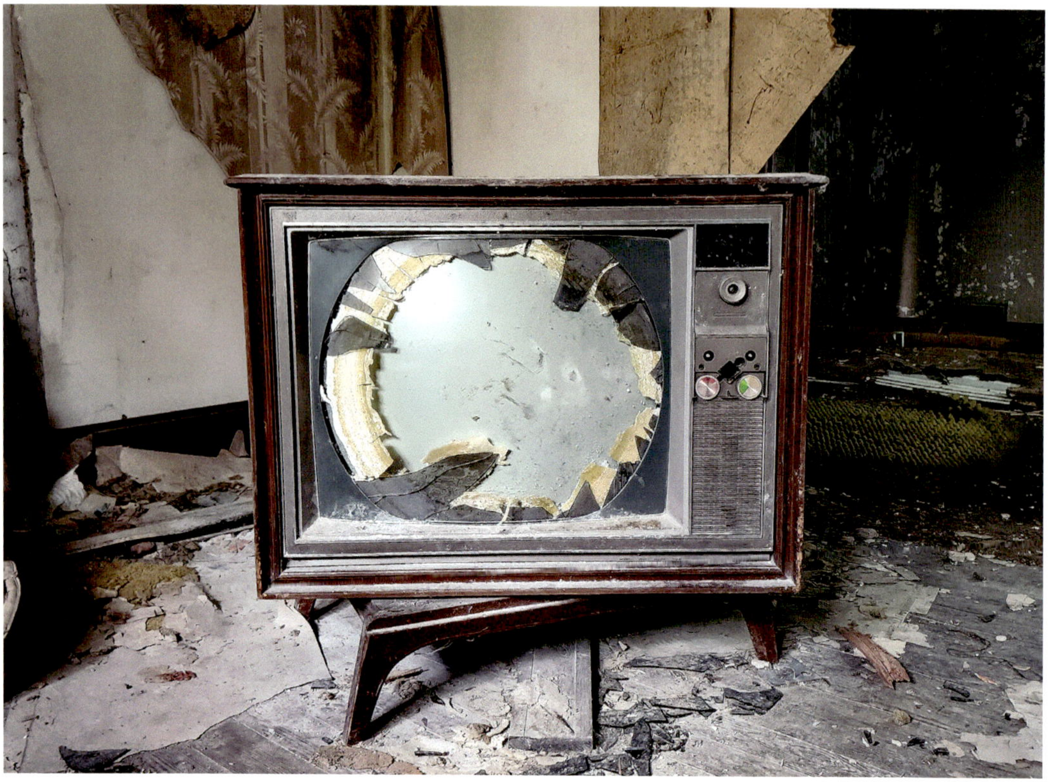

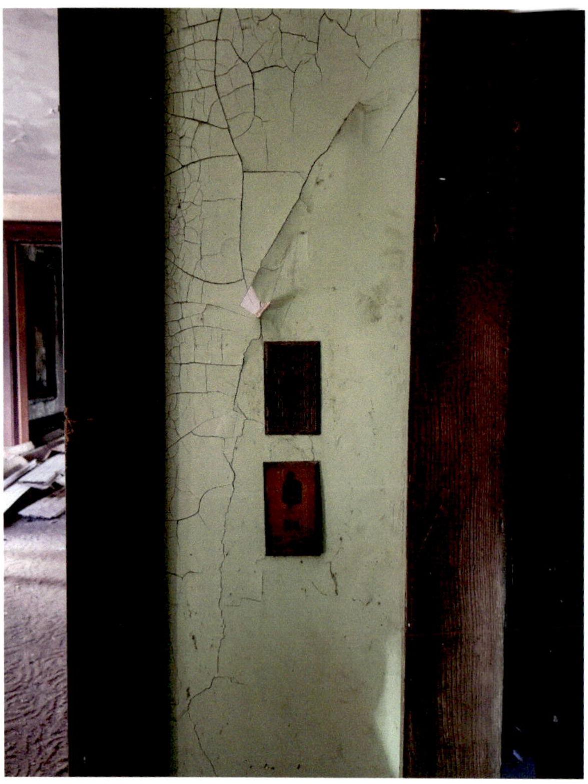

Above: This angle gives a better vantage of the wallpaper, hardwood floors, television, and doorway to the hall.

Left: Light switch and outlets on the outer wall between the stairs and the living room.

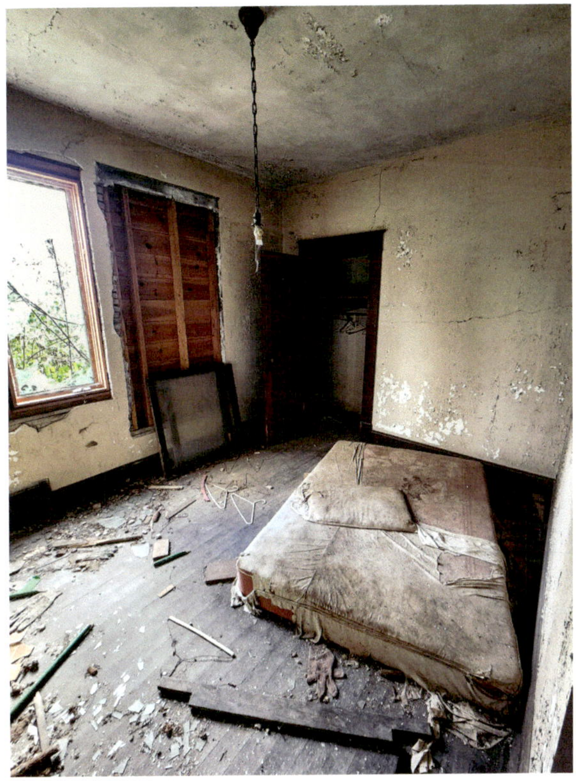

In one of the bedrooms, the only things left behind were an old, stained mattress with a fitted sheet, a pillow, and various hangers.

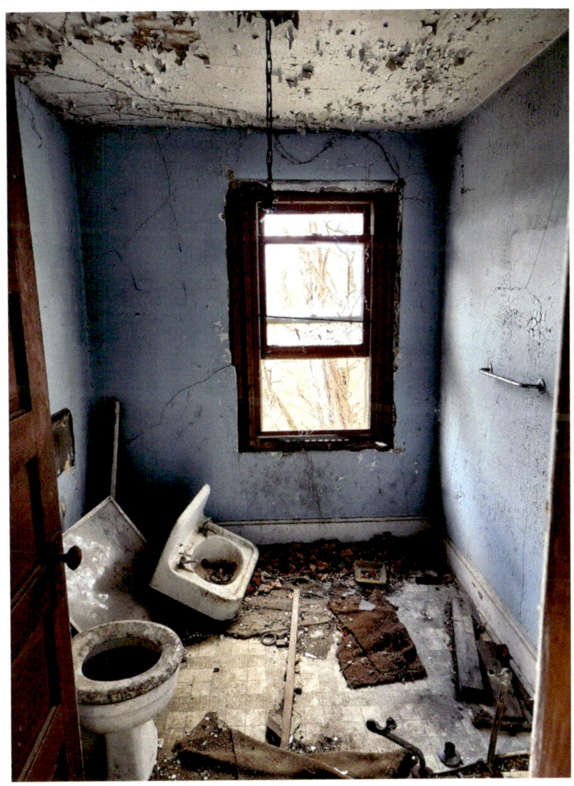

The upstairs bathroom looked as though it was in the process of being either remodeled or salvaged when someone decided to give up on it.

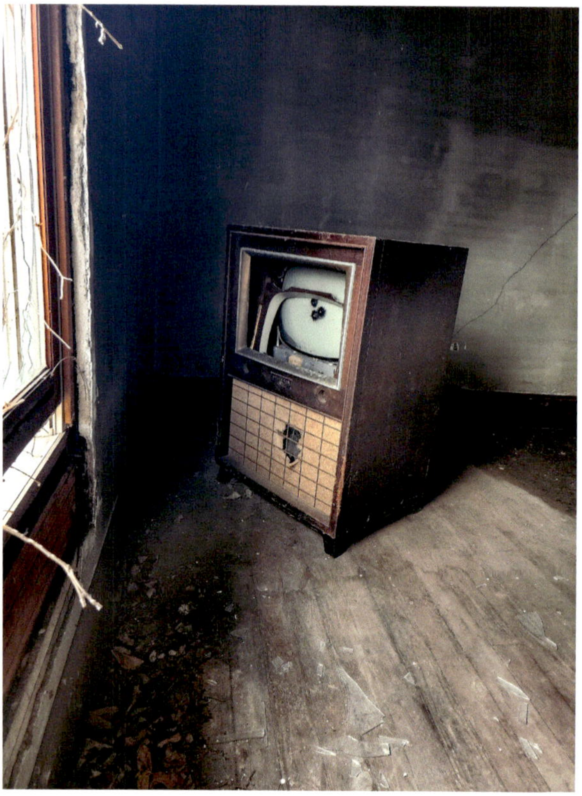

Left: The second bedroom only had a solitary broken television left behind next to the window.

Below: Old farmhouses are a common sight when driving through the Midwest. Sometimes the farm buildings are still in use, while the house itself no longer serves a real purpose.

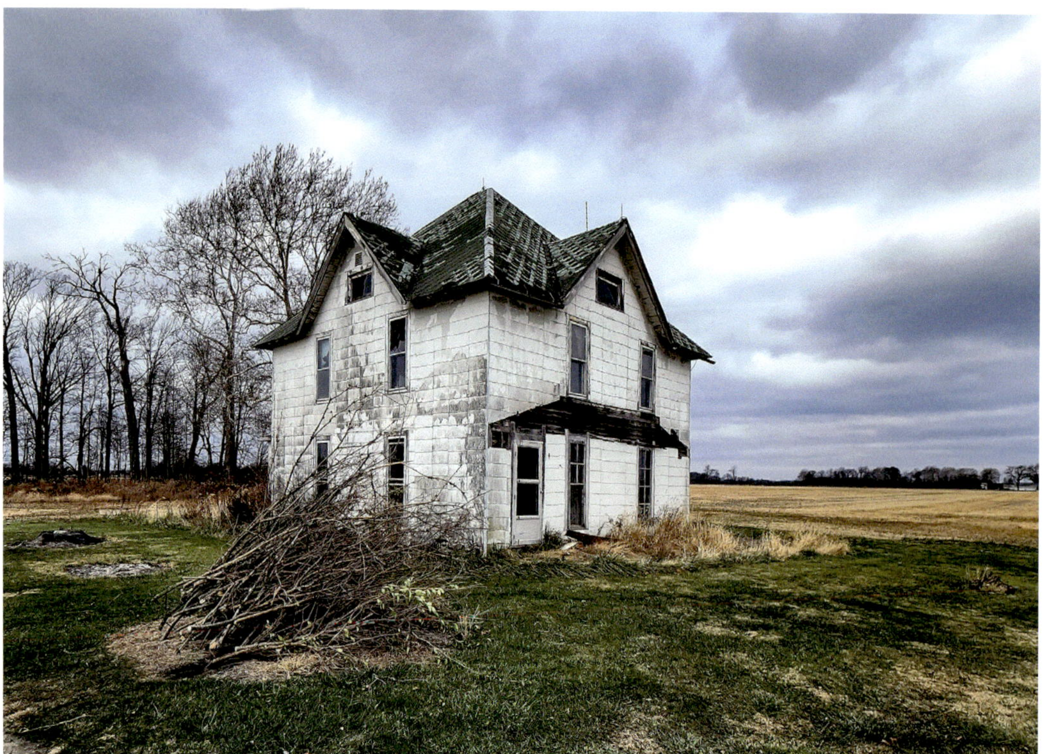

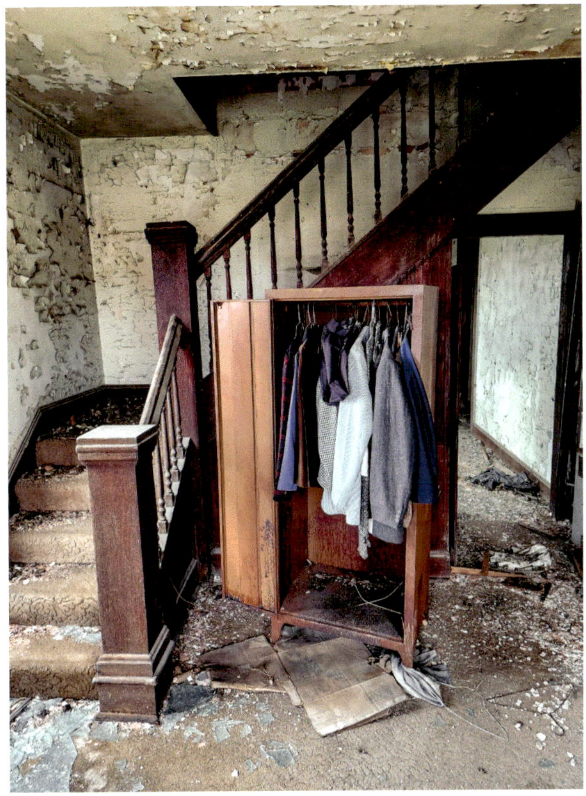

Right: There was a wardrobe left directly in the front windows of the house.

Below: The fireplace in the main room had been covered at some point, but I absolutely love the different types of wallpaper.

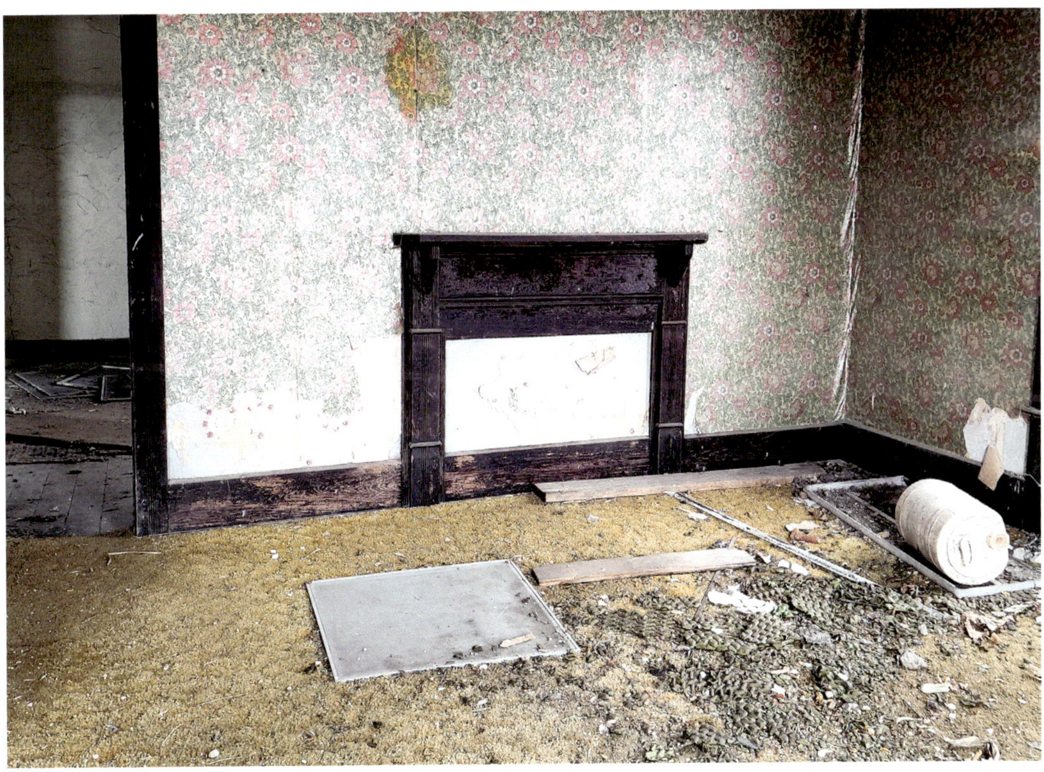

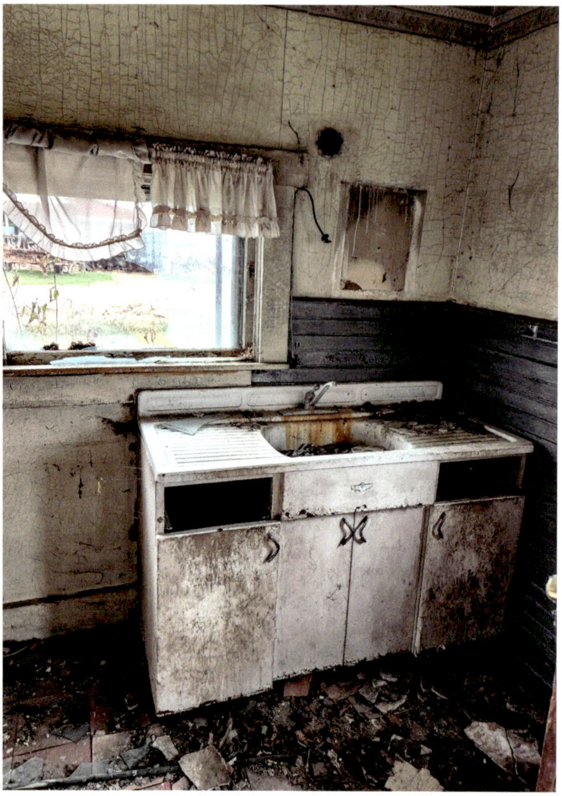

The kitchen sink, which overlooks the side of the house. I especially like finding curtains or window treatments still hanging.

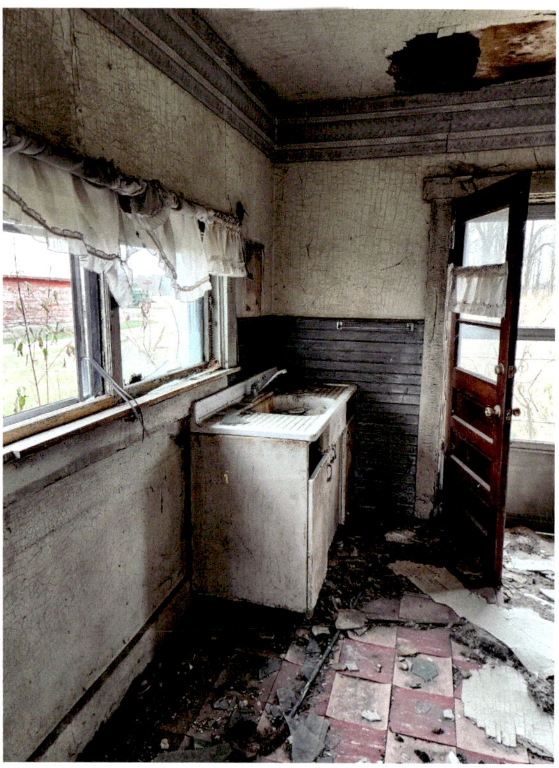

The back door was also left completely open inside, but the storm door was closed securely. The colorful tiles were an excellent touch.

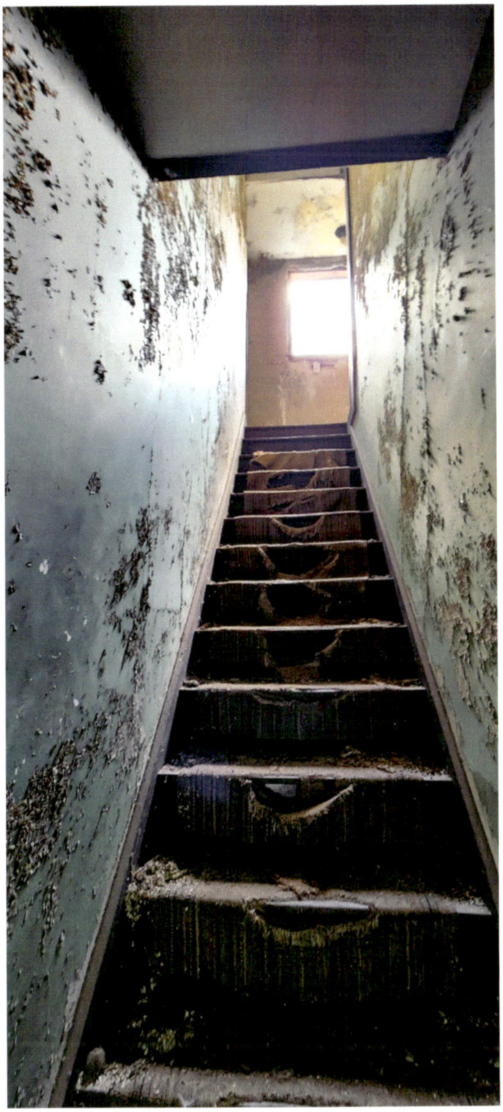

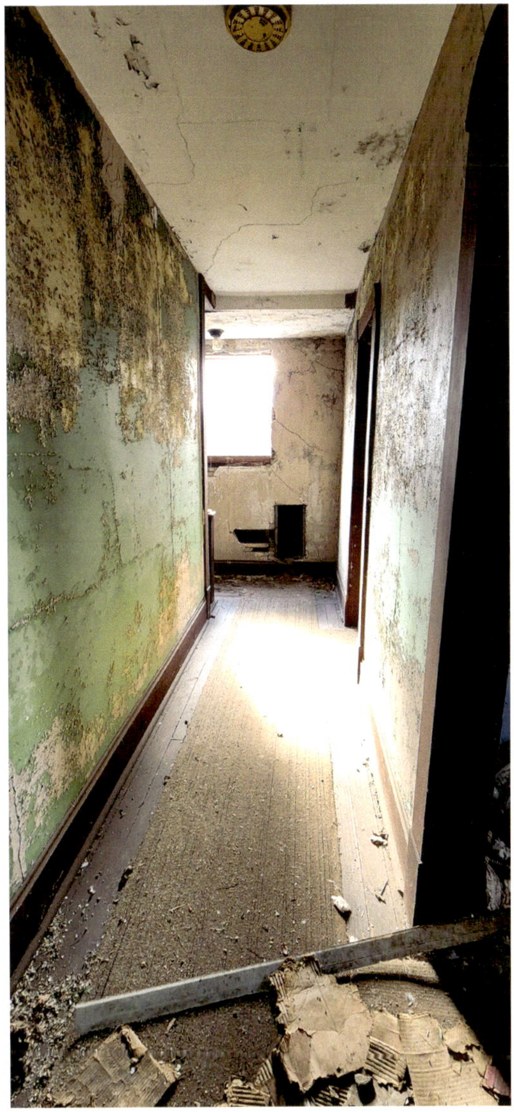

Above left: Stairs with the carpet worn down to the wood over the years.

Above right: The upstairs hallway with paint peeling from years of neglect.

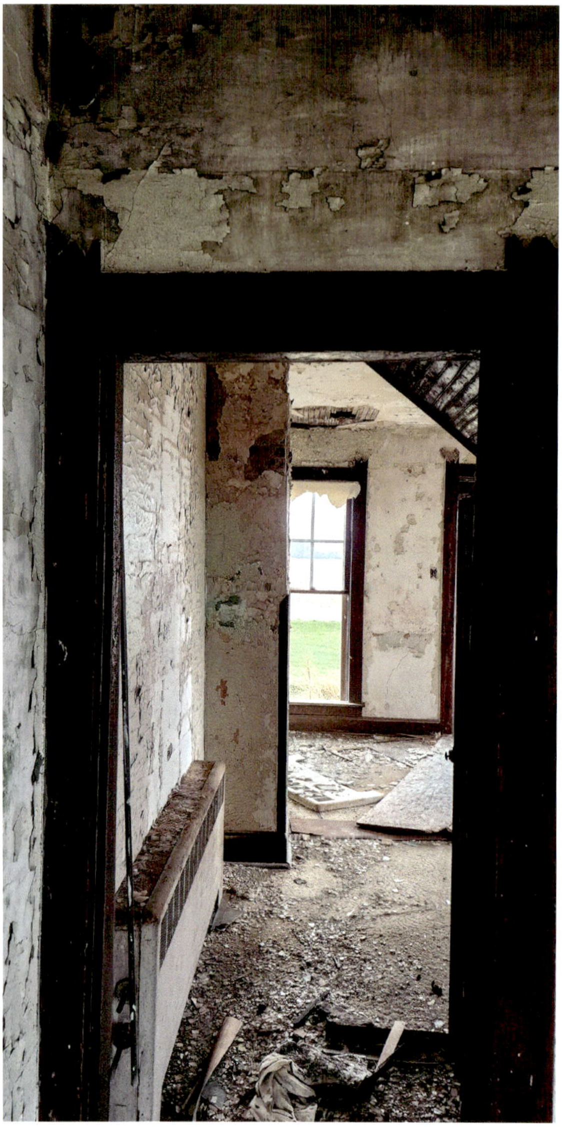

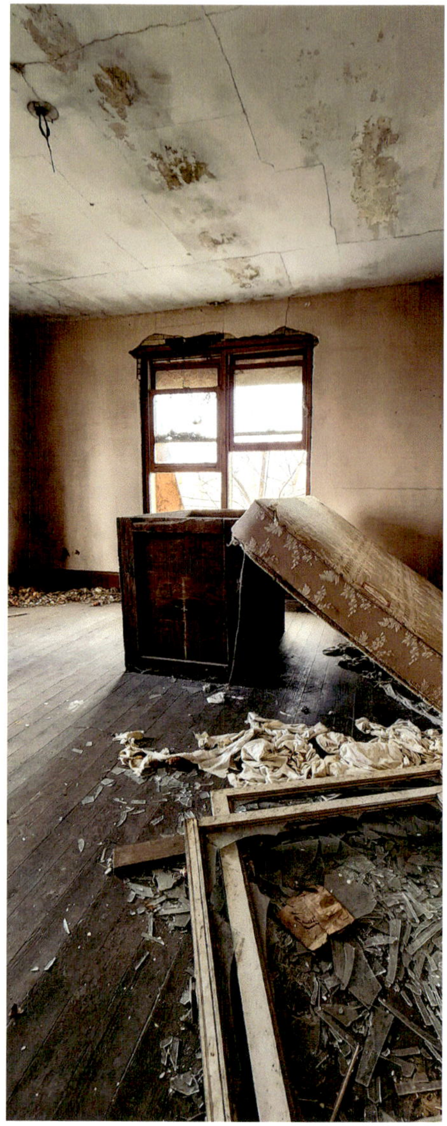

Above left: The entrance to one of the upstairs bedrooms.

Above right: A large empty crate, some broken windows, and an old mattress were left behind.

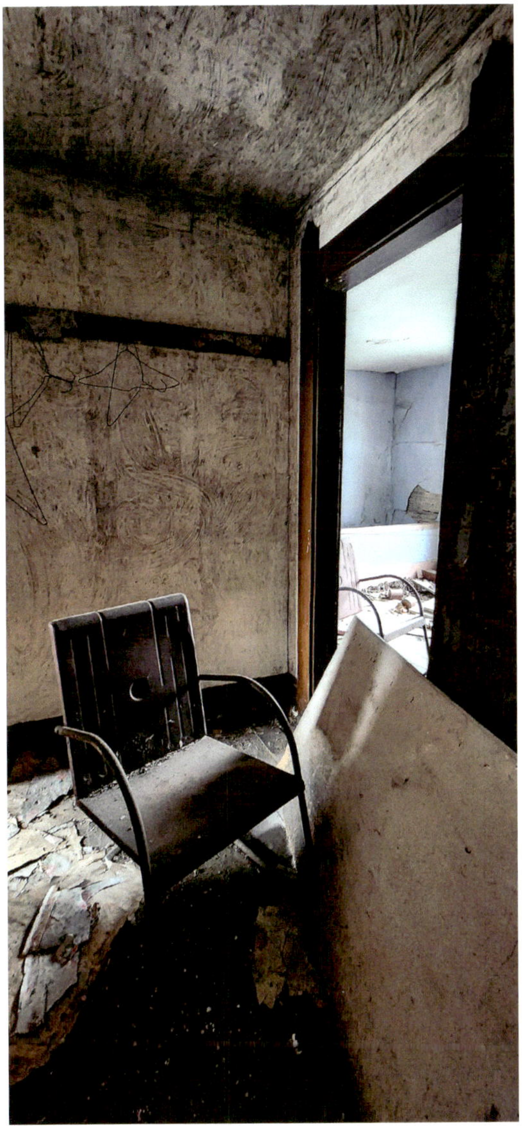

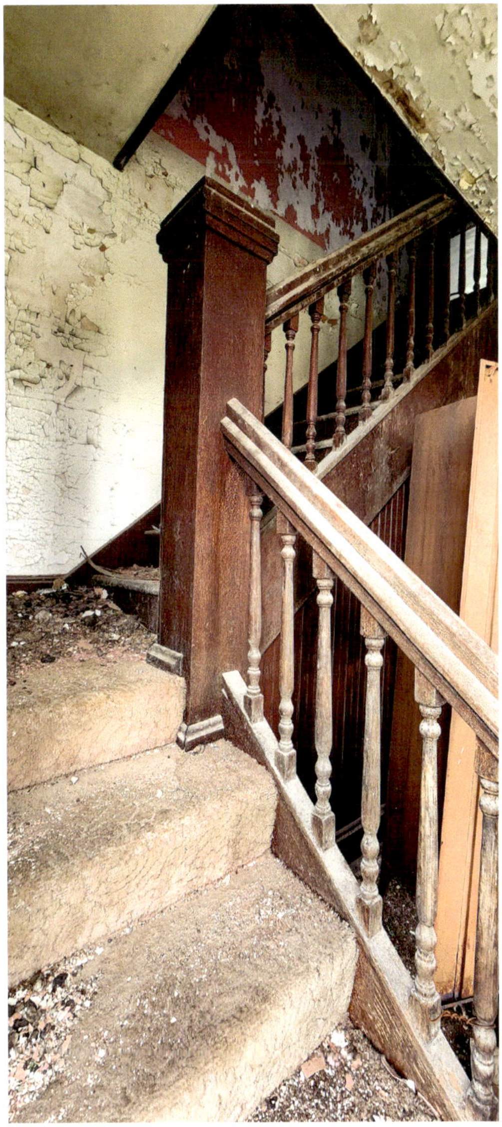

Above left: The entrance to the second bedroom, which was full of animal excrement.

Above right: The entrance staircase had some fantastic woodwork.

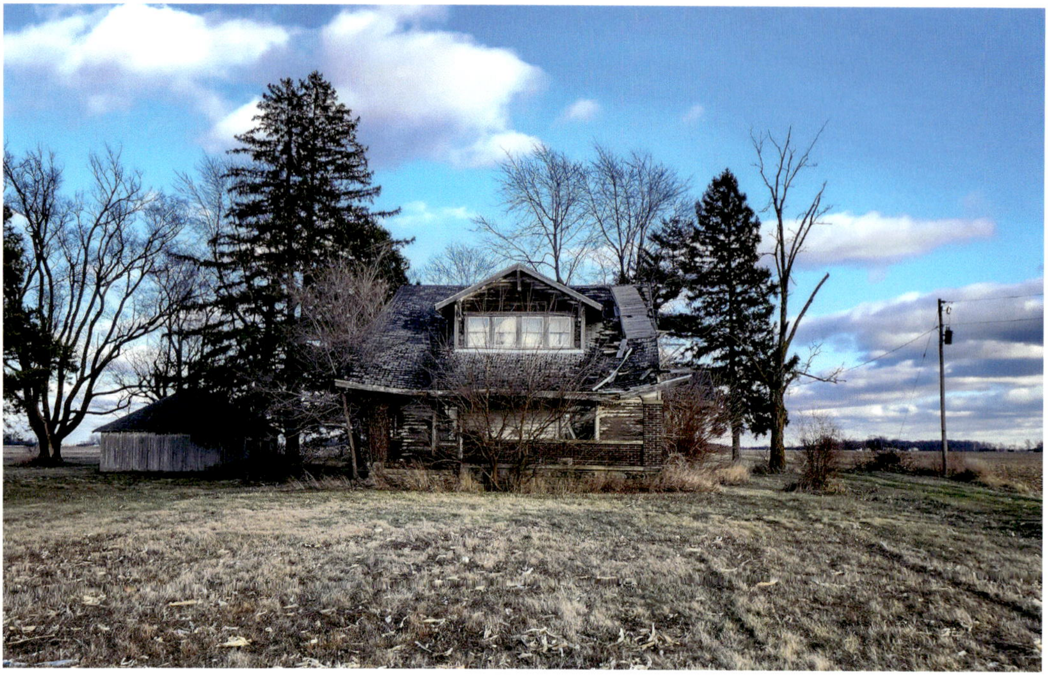

We spotted this beautiful house from a distance once harvest had been completed.

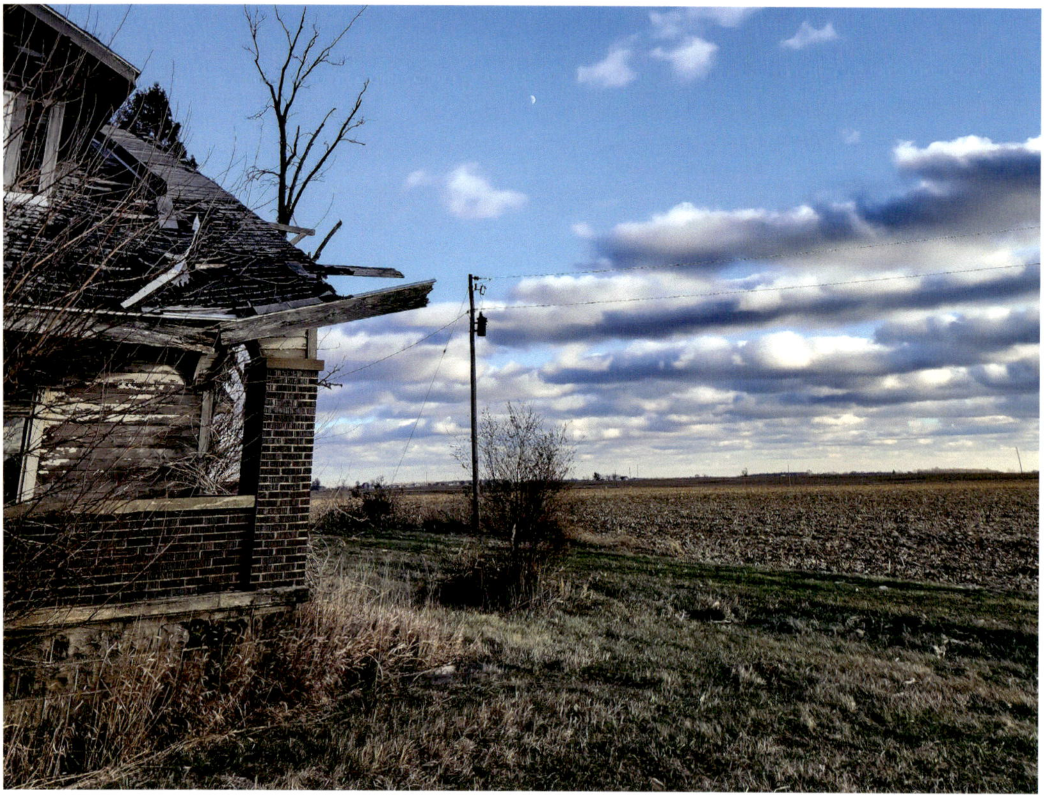

A very isolated area and a lot of roof damage.

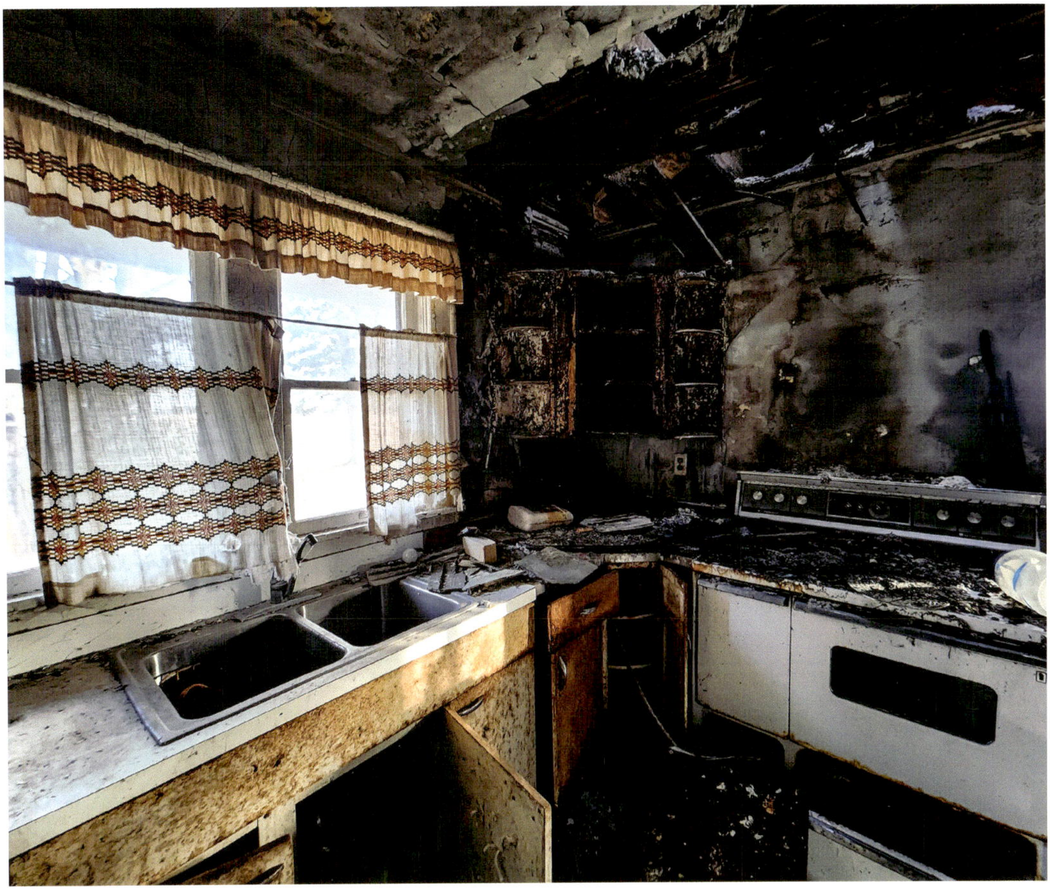

Judging from the scorched remains, the kitchen is the point of origin for the roof damage.

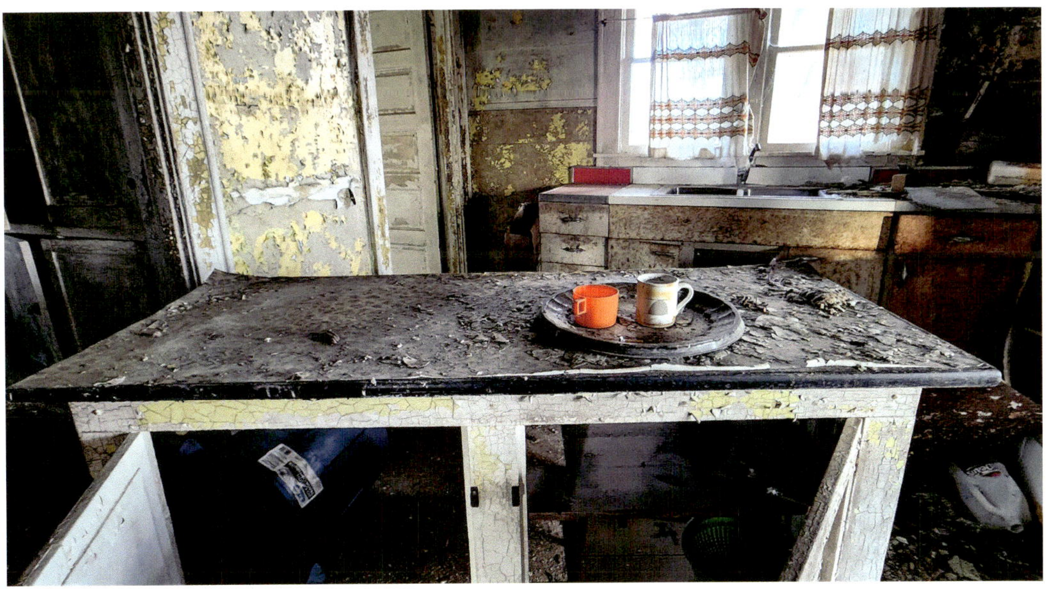

Dishes left behind on a rolling cabinet.

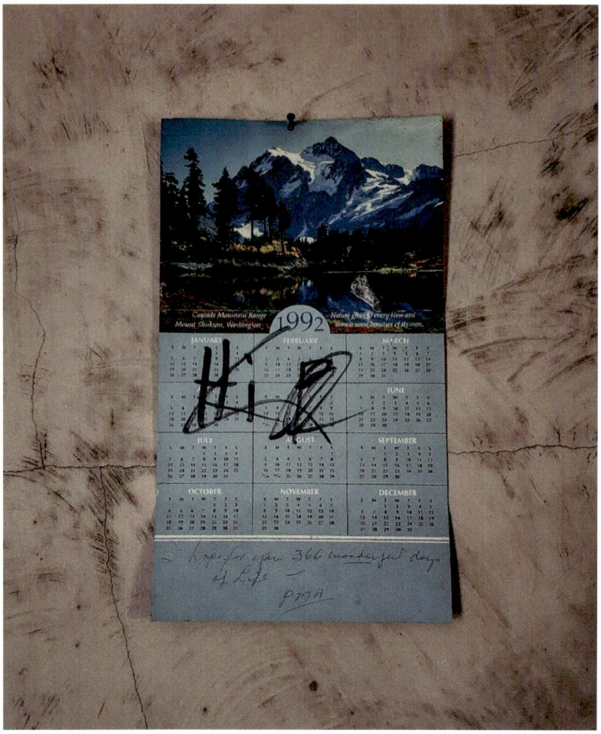

Calendar from 1992, a leap year.

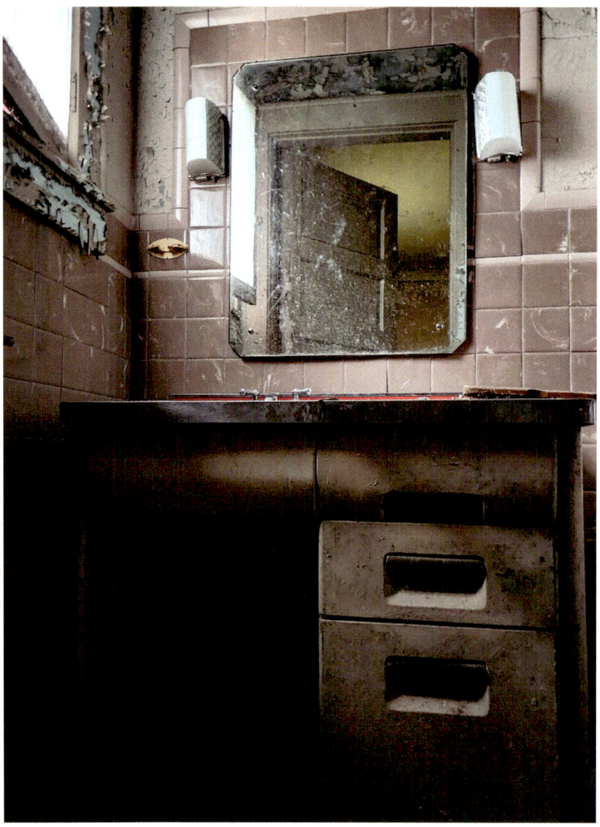

This pink bathroom was everything; the tile was in incredible condition.

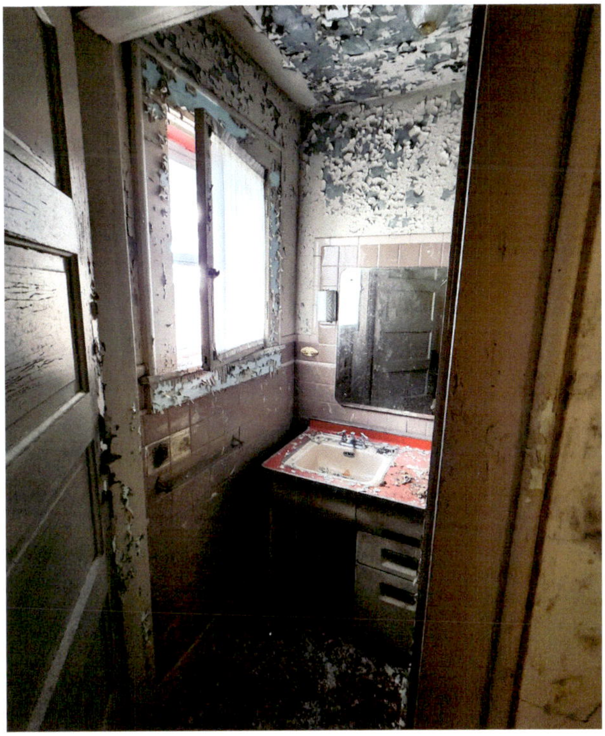

A full shot of the bathroom vanity. The light pink paint has started peeling, showing the former blue and teal colors.

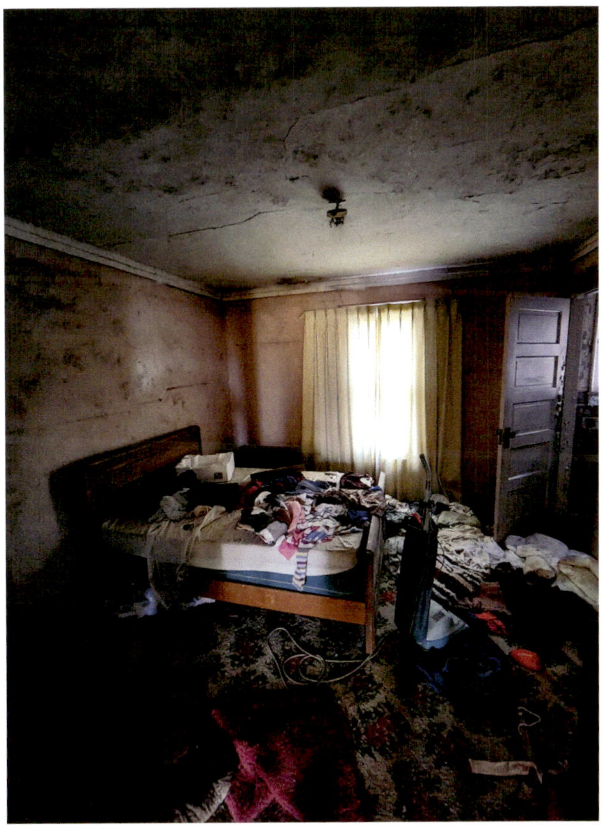

A bed with clothes still piled on top and a vacuum left out from its last cleaning.

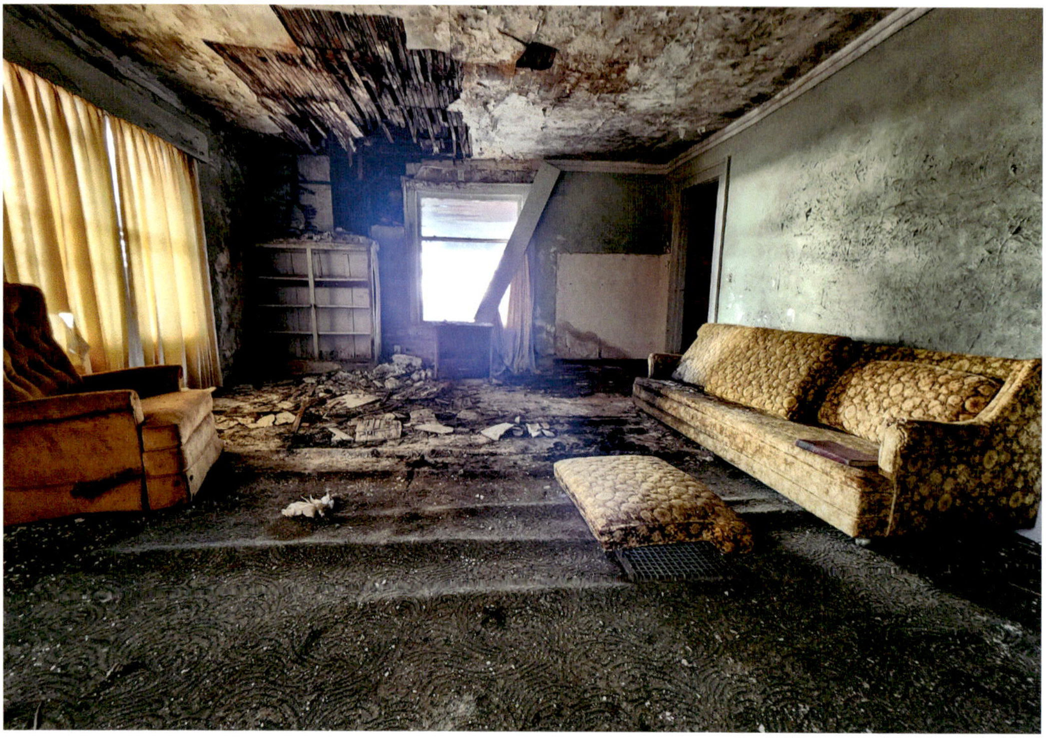

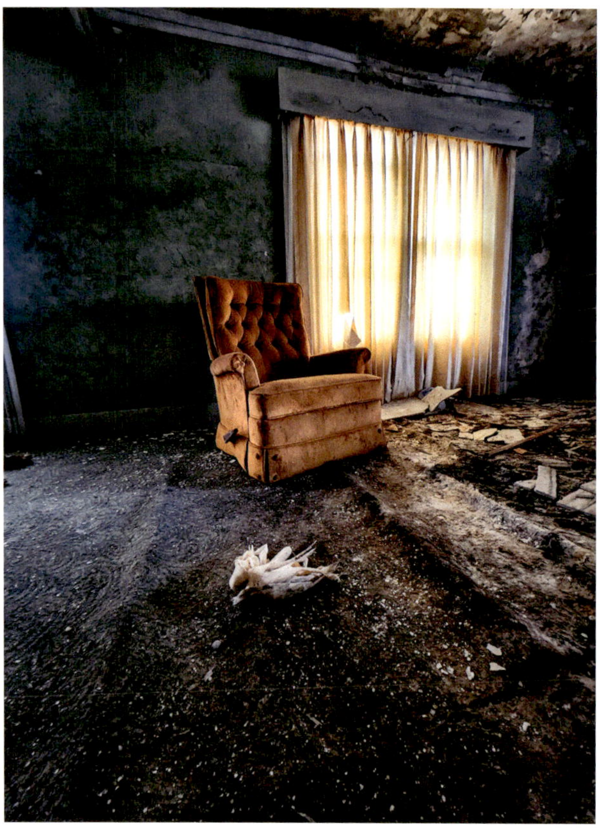

Above: The living room featuring very 70s furniture.

Left: A recliner and a piece of corn sit at the edge of the decayed floor.

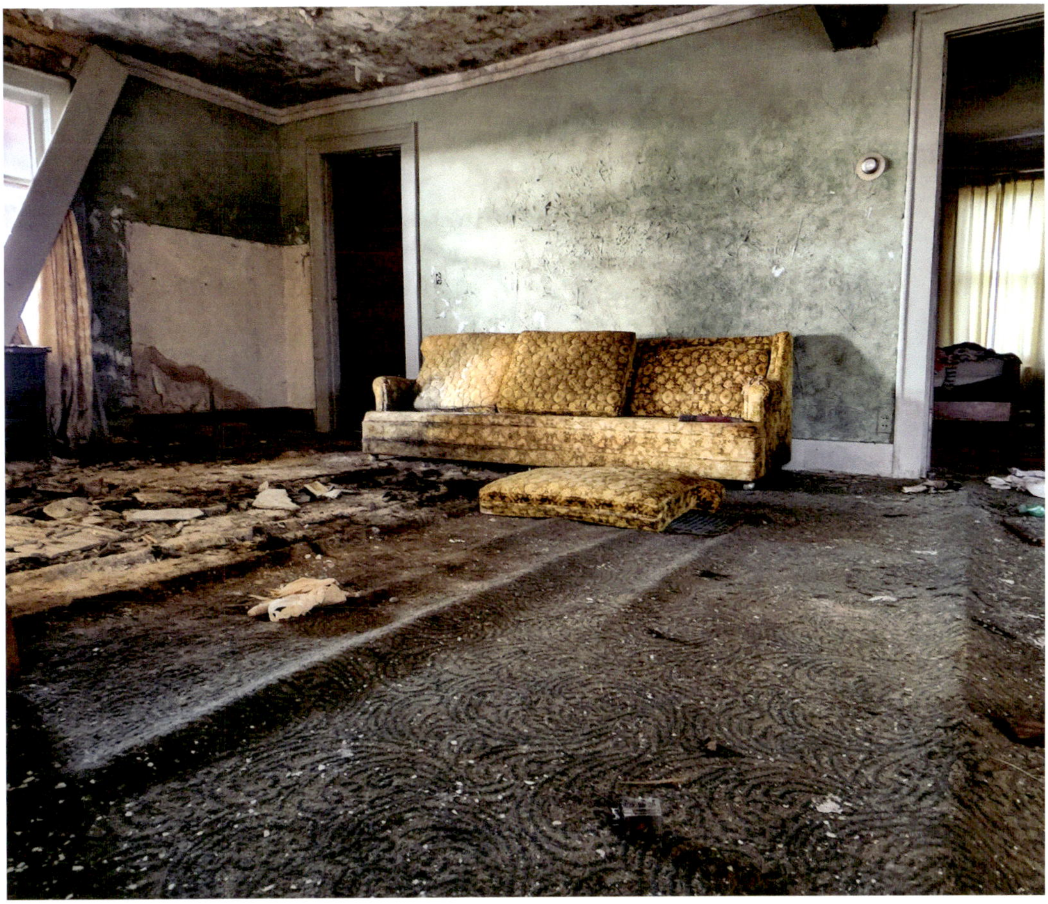

This part of the house had very unstable flooring.

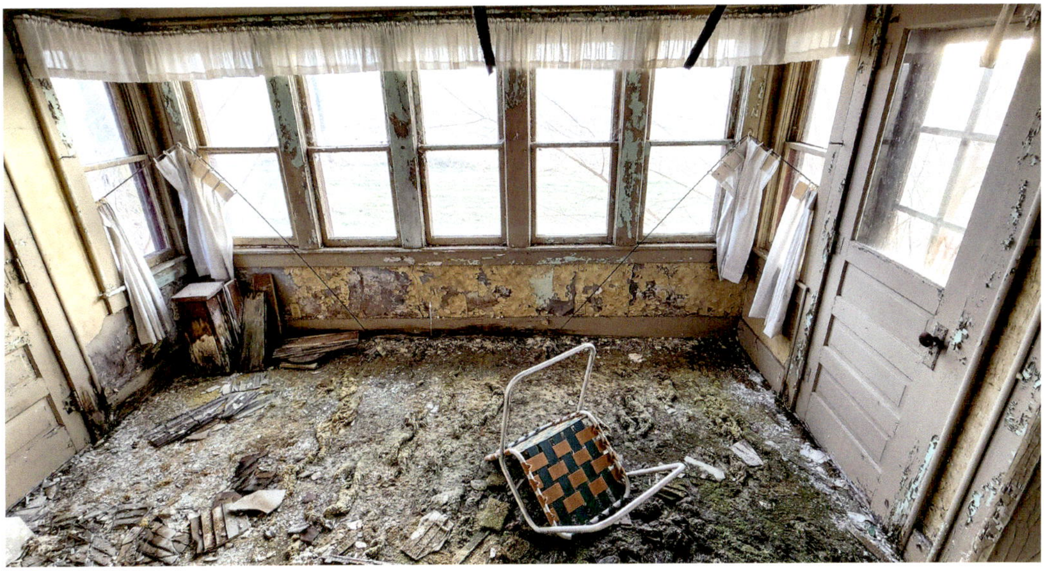

The mud room, which is where I assume they stored the things they were not planning on taking with them.

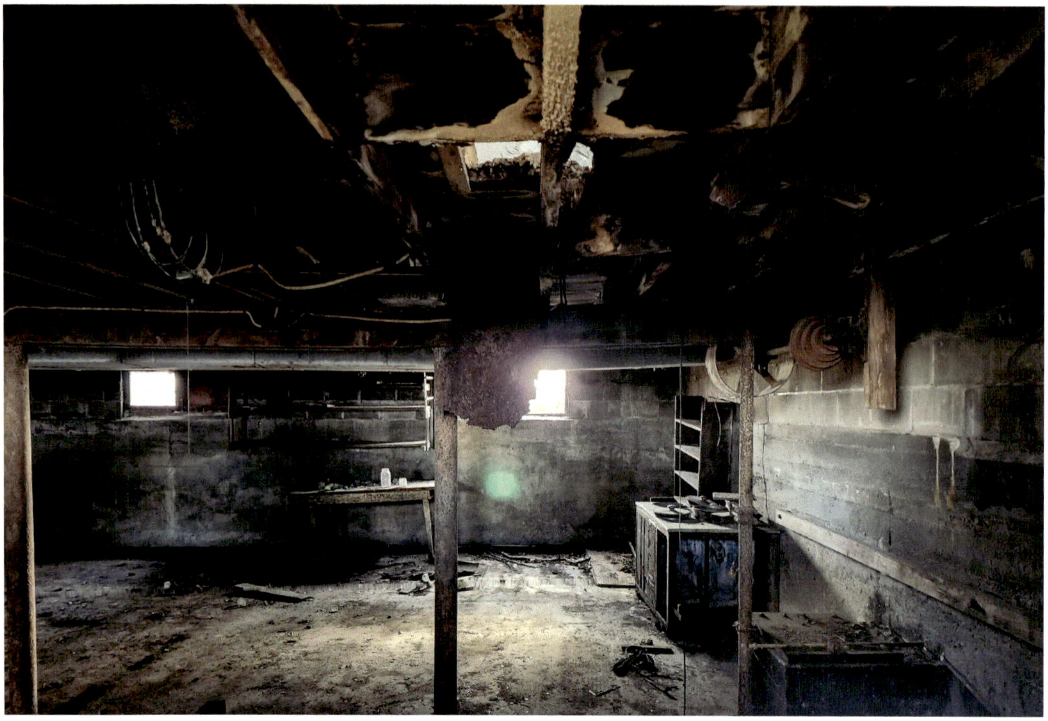

The basement, as photographed from a broken window outside.

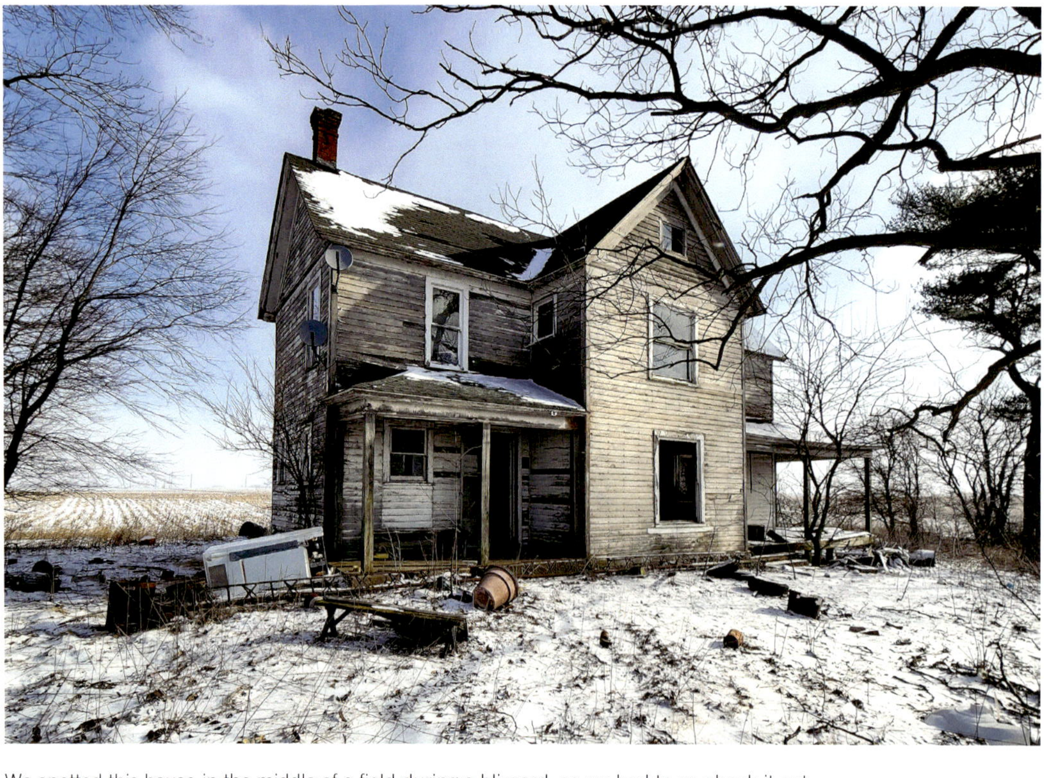

We spotted this house in the middle of a field during a blizzard, so we had to go check it out.

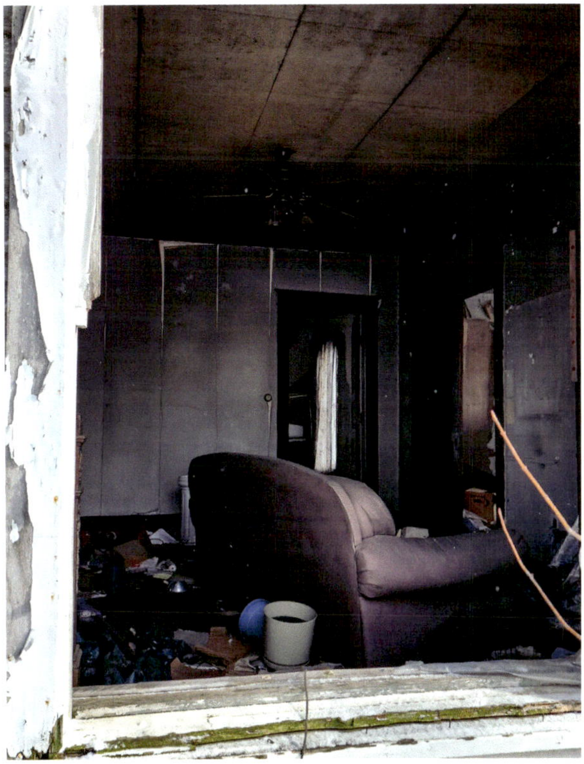

Looking in through the windows, we could tell that no one had been around here for a good while.

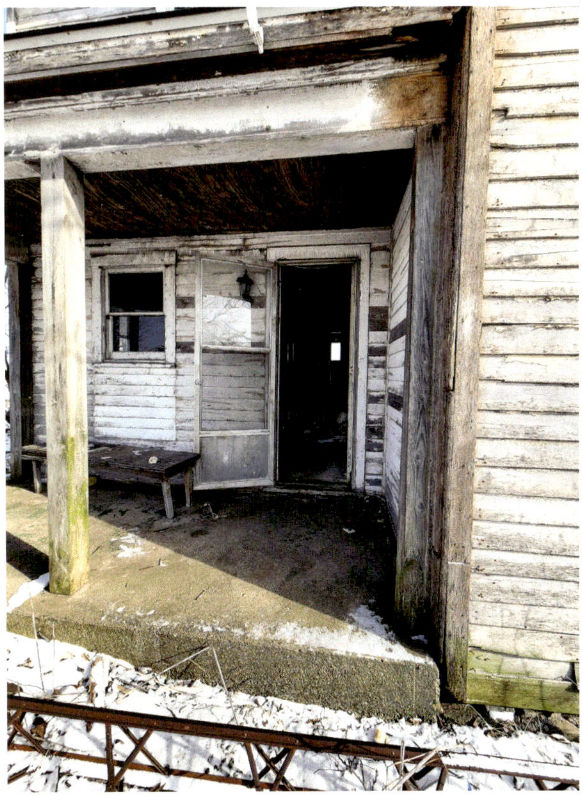

The front door was left wide open, but the glass was still intact.

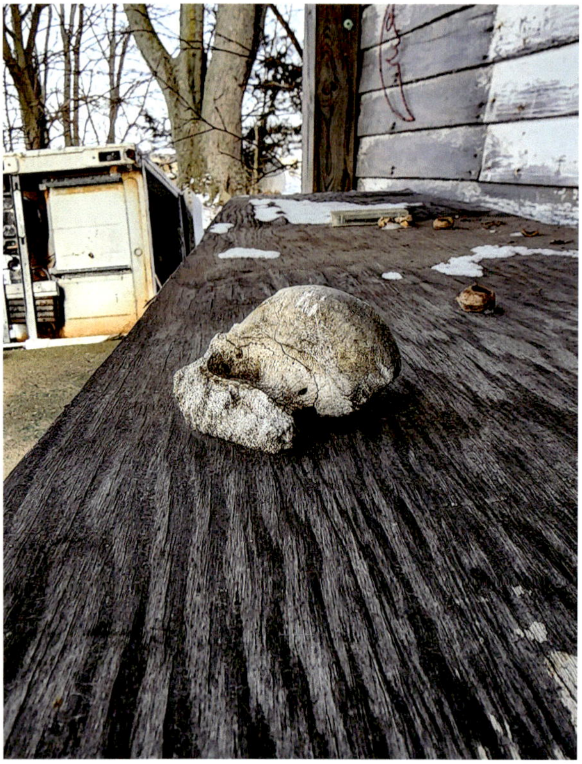

A miscellaneous piece of bone left on the table outside of the house. There is some junked industrial equipment behind it.

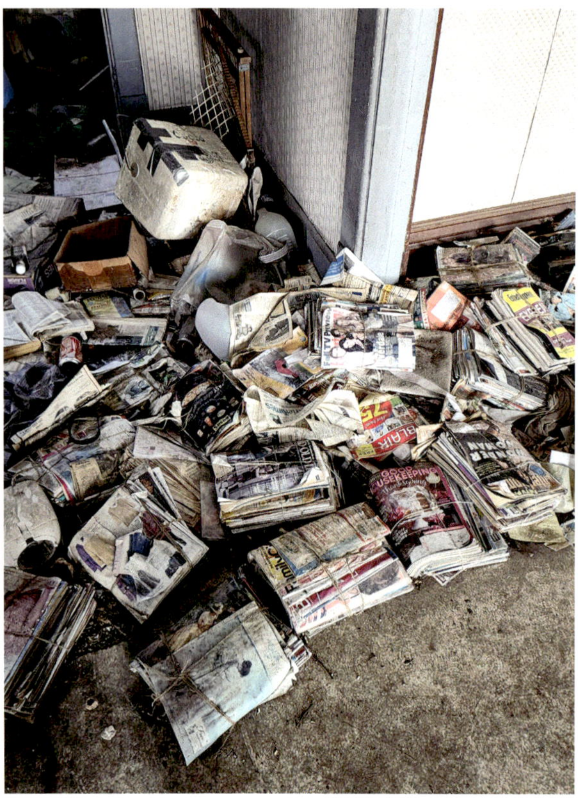

There were piles and piles of bundled magazines near the entrance to what was once the laundry/utility room.

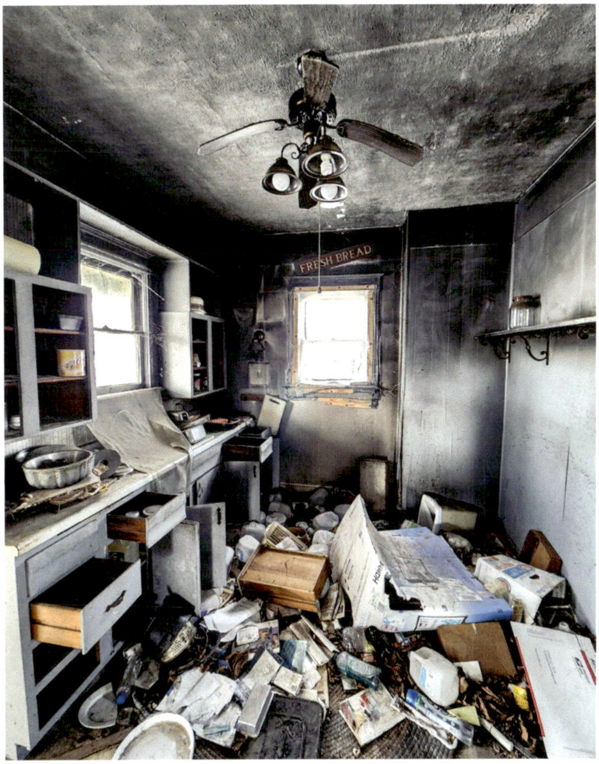

The kitchen looks to have had smoke damage at one point, but the shelves still held Tupperware and various dry ingredients.

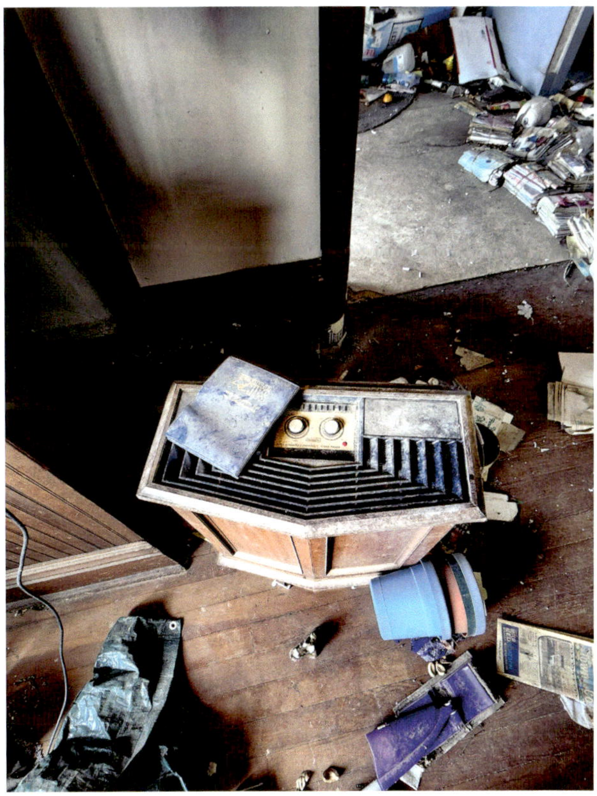

I am unsure of whether this old Sears appliance was an air conditioner or a dehumidifier of some sort. There is an old tradeshow book on top of it.

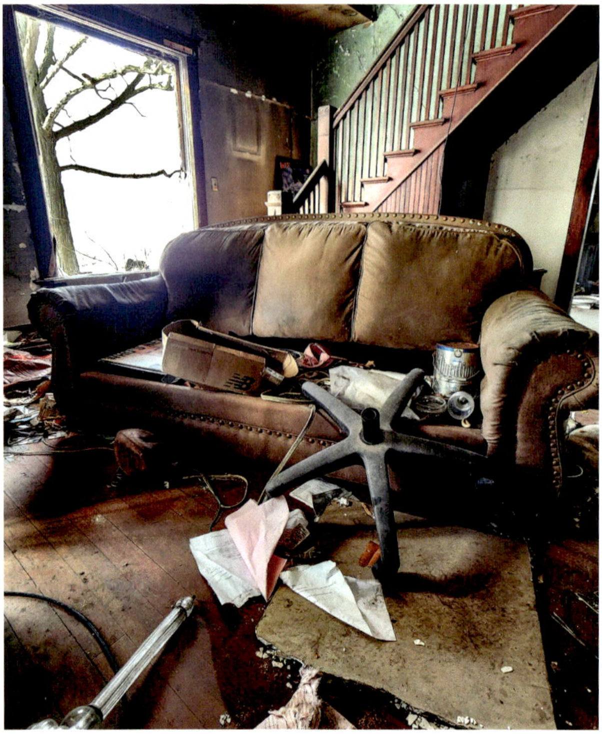

The cushions had been removed from the couch at some point, and it was piled with junk and broken furniture parts.

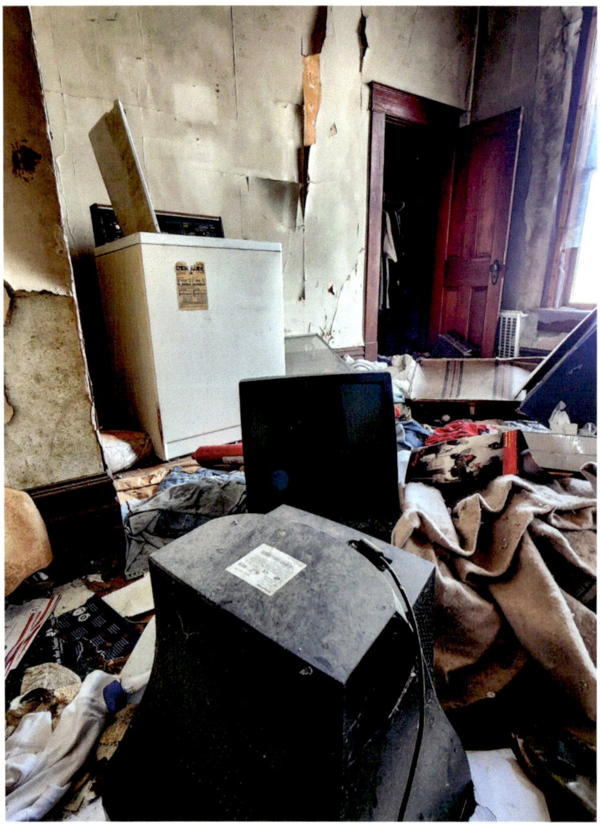

The washer was left open, and there were multiple televisions laying on the clothing that littered the ground.

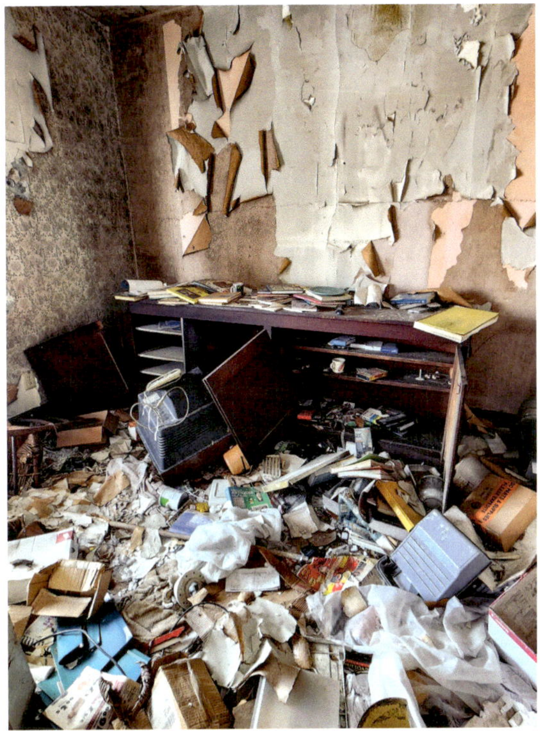

Right: Even though it had started peeling, the wallpaper above the desk was still beautiful. There was another television laying on the floor.

Below: A 1970s-style recliner that was in the front room. The bulletin board still contains a former Purdue University sport schedule.

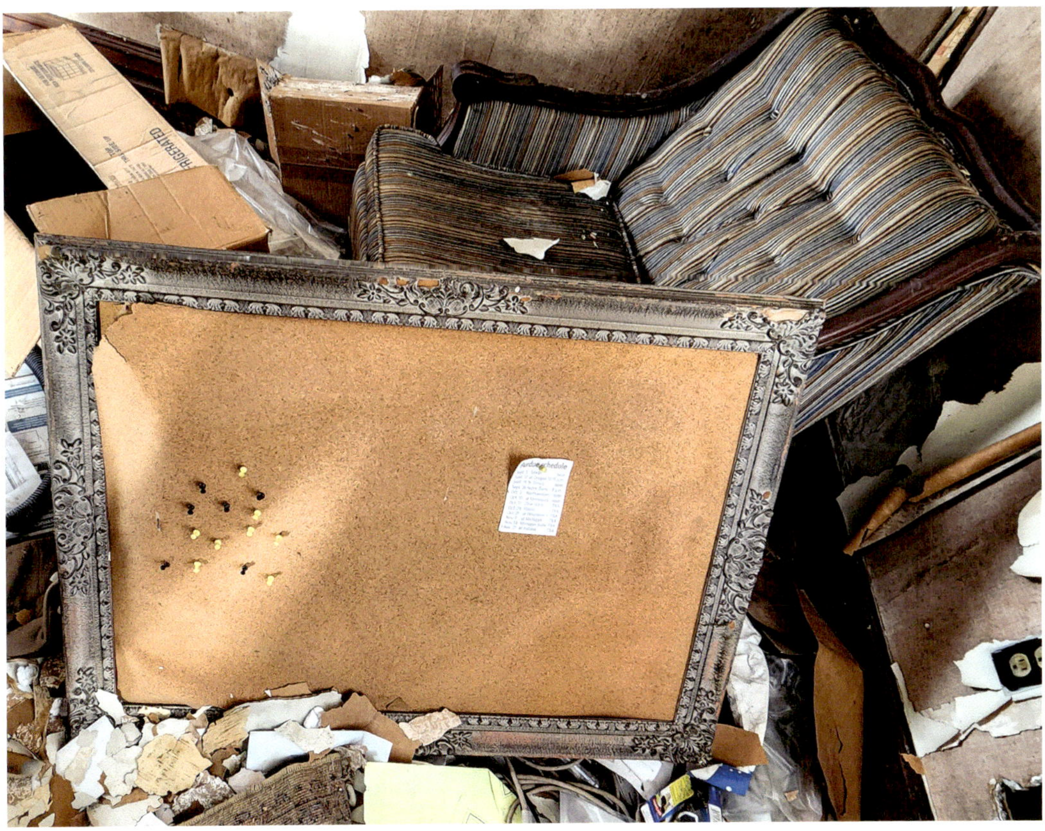

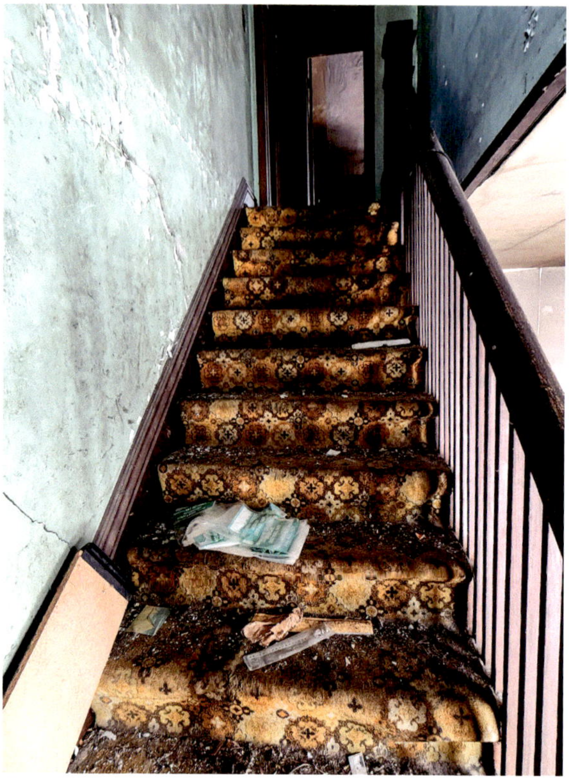

The carpet on these stairs was fantastically mid-century;there was also an entire set of small bank bags laying on them.

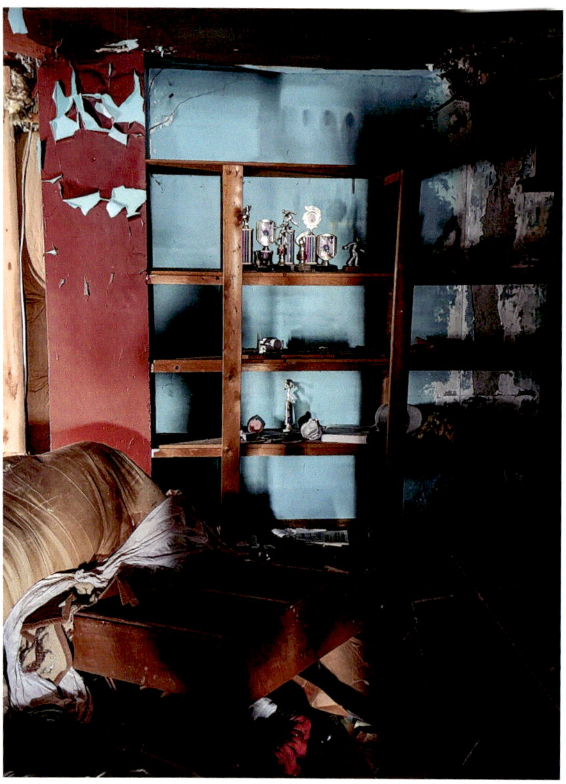

The built-in shelves here housed an array of bowling trophies that ended up being left behind.

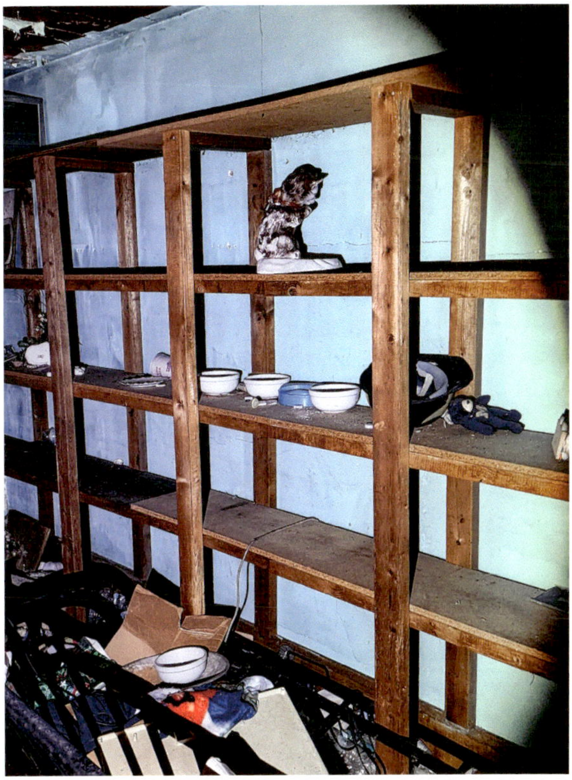

The other side of the room housed various bowls and knickknacks. I'm pretty certain my great grandmother owned a similar cat statue.

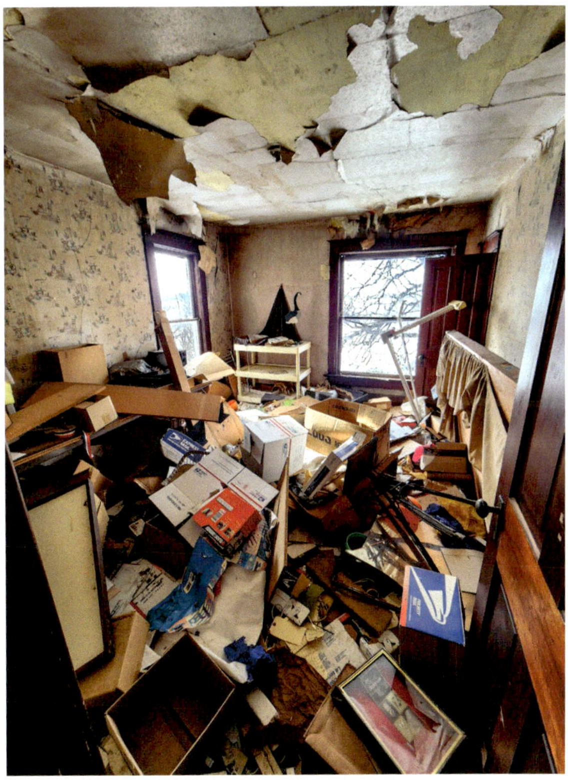

Various boxes and collector paraphernalia litter the floor in the second bedroom. It was packed so full, we did not feel safe attempting to get to the closet.

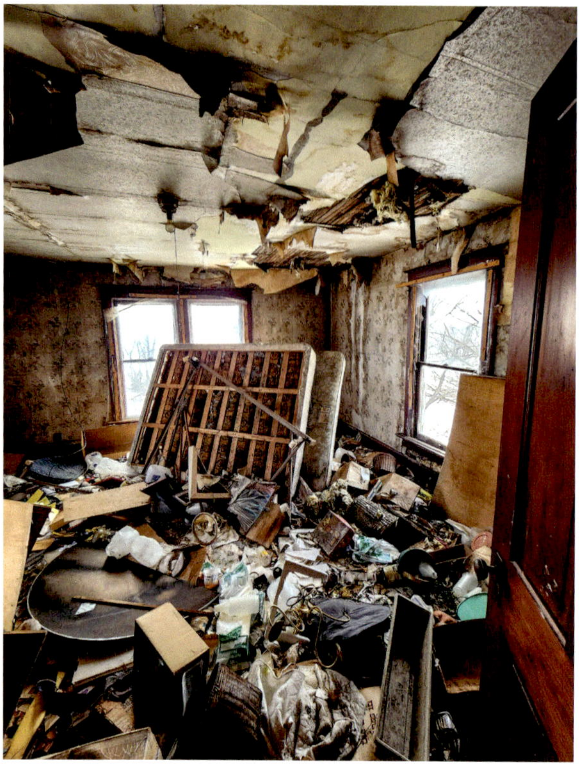

The last bedroom shows how much the passage of time has taken its toll on the house. The ceiling has started buckling and there is a ton of mold everywhere.

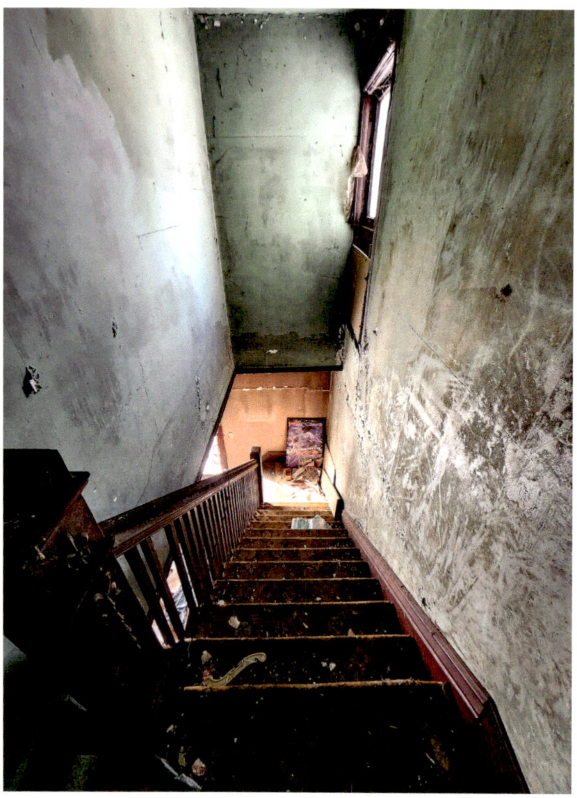

A shot going down the stairs showing the window at the top and how much more inviting the main floor seems from the top.

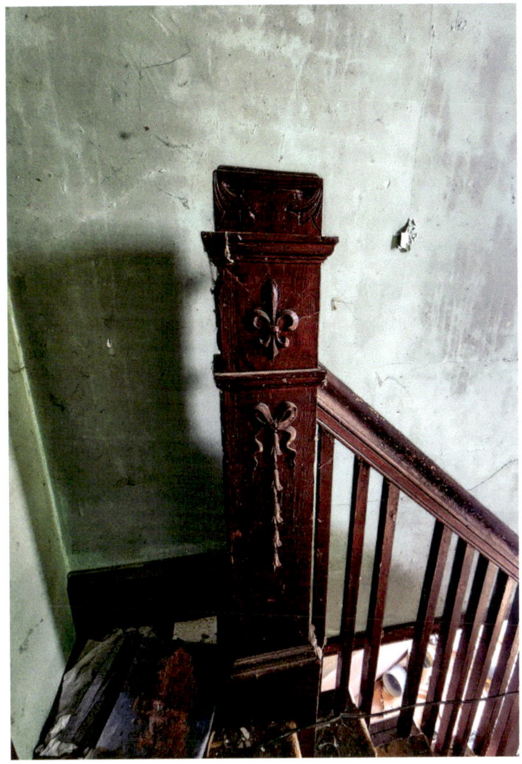

The details on the staircase were exquisite and have held up well over time. I'm very surprised that animals hadn't damaged any of the wood.

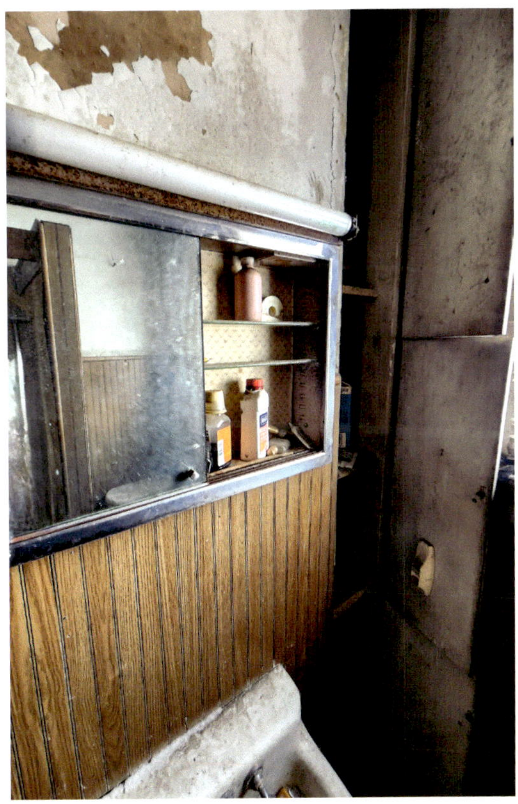

Everything was left in the medicine cabinet in the bathroom. The floor had long ago collapsed, so I had to get creative to check it out.

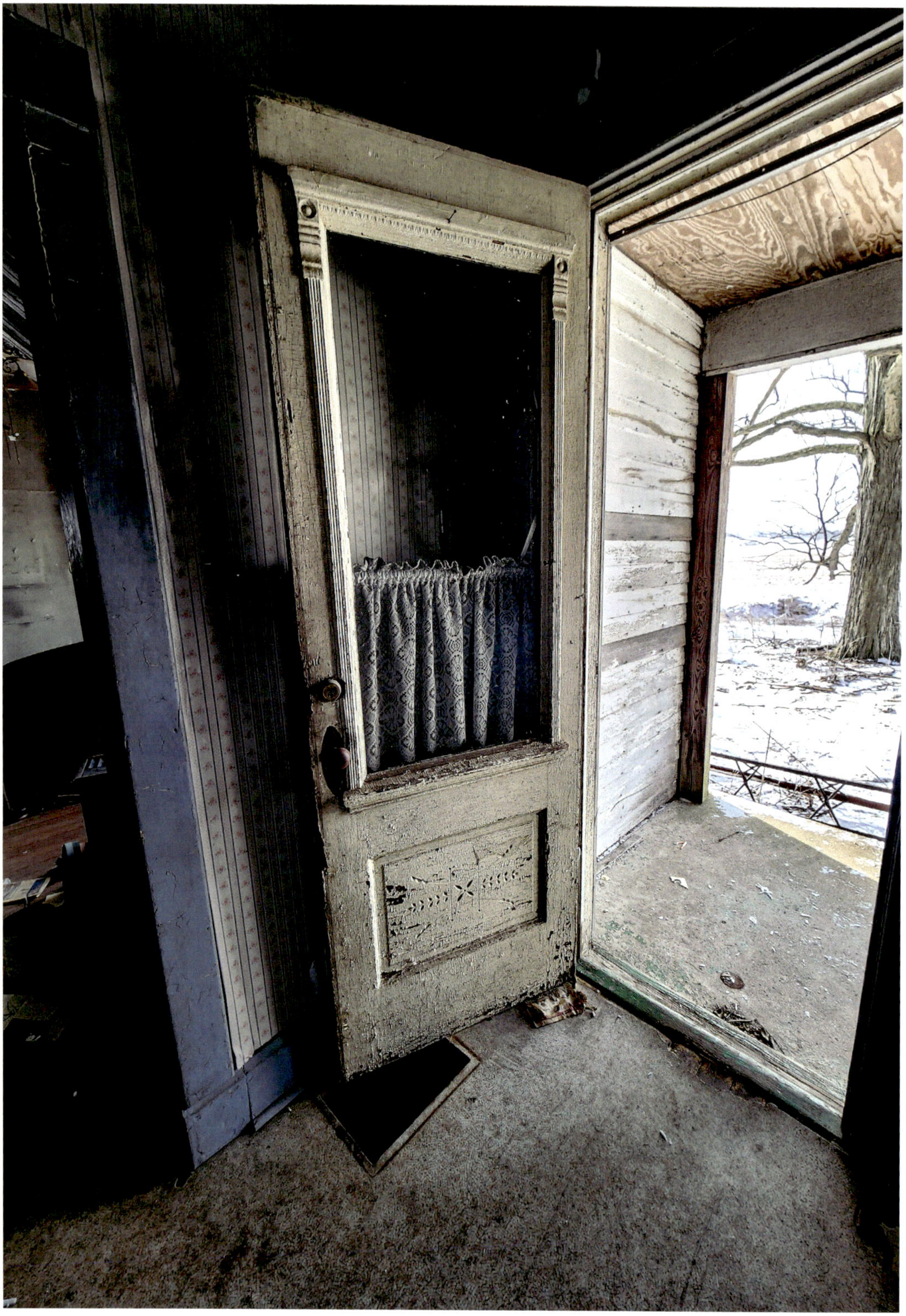

The front door also has incredible hand-carved details that have held up incredibly well considering it has been left to the elements for so long.

4

EDUCATION IN EARLY INDIANA

Hoosier pioneers had little access to education in the early part of the nineteenth century. The advancement of the family's financial situation was the main concern, as it was in so many other facets of pioneer life. Children learned the fundamentals of farm life from their parents, including how to hunt, build a shelter, cultivate and harvest crops, spin and sew fabric, and cook. Additionally, parents may have taught their kids to read, write a few words, such as their names, and use basic arithmetic. Children might learn and practice reading and writing at church and in Sunday school. The Bible would have been one of the only books that a Hoosier pioneer child ever read given the lack of books in those days. There were no secular, or nonreligious, educational options in Indiana. Progress was initially slow to nonexistent despite the state constitution's 1816 commitment to establish a general education system that would be accessible to all inhabitants. Similar to today's public schools, common schools were founded locally and received funding from the town or township rather than the state. They were not accessible to everyone and never free. State standards and teacher-training programs were nonexistent. Teachers' skill levels therefore varied significantly, and they were paid very little. Less than 25% of children in Indiana between the ages of five and fifteen were enrolled in school, according to the federal census of 1840. In addition, around one in seven adult Hoosiers were illiterate. In the Union's twenty-eight states, Indiana came in at number eighteen in terms of literacy. The low levels of education in the Upland South, which had been the home of many Hoosier pioneers, contributed in part to Indiana's high illiteracy rate. However, in a broader sense, the state's illiteracy was due to its failure to uphold the promise of universally free education.

Education reformers launched a vigorous push to establish a true system of public education after the 1840 census served as a call to action. A missionary from New England named Caleb Mills was committed to bringing both religion and education to the frontier. Graduate of Andover Theological Seminary and Dartmouth College, he traveled to Crawfordsville in 1833 to lead a Presbyterian institution that would later become Wabash College. Before the 1840 census exposed the unpleasant facts about Hoosier education, Mills had been a supporter of public education. However, when the report was out, he became the main proponent of a state system of public education. Mills, who simply signed his writings "One of the People," penned and distributed six persuasive letters to the state assembly between 1846 and 1852. They are possibly the most significant texts on Indiana's educational system ever produced. He cited "a lack of qualified teachers, appropriate school materials, a proper level of community interest in the subject, adequate funding, and the way of obtaining such monies" as the reasons for Indiana's educational lag. There is only one way to ensure good schools, and that is to pay for them, he said in support of the need for state and township school taxes. (Madison and Sandweiss)

The General Assembly of Indiana submitted a statewide referendum under pressure from Mills and other reformers, asking eligible voters to decide whether to enact taxes sufficient to provide at least three months of free public school education for all children. The 1849 referendum was successful, though not by a wide margin. The referendum featured a flaw that made it necessary for a majority of voters in each county to accept it before it would take effect there. It was approved by sixty-one counties and rejected by twenty-nine. The development of a statewide common school system was hampered by this conflicting response. These initiatives had an impact on the 1851 Indiana Constitution, which created a system of common schools and led to the adoption of the 1852 Free School Law. The 1852 statute required counties throughout the state to set up a system to offer at least three months of free common-school education. In order to fund public education evenly across the state, the law also imposed a state tax. This statute did not have a provision that would have allowed individual counties to opt out, unlike the 1849 act. In 1854, Mills was appointed as the second superintendent of the state's public schools. (Madison and Sandweiss)

Many of Indiana's early settlers saw state-supported education as a step toward a more centralized government; they reasoned that this would result in less local control over communities and eventually in the loss of individual freedom, whereas many school supporters saw education as a way to ensure equal opportunity for all Hoosiers. Some settlers even asserted that taxes were the biggest impediment to their belief that they had a divinely granted freedom to pursue riches. Regardless of how the schools were funded, formal education was not always welcomed since some pioneers believed it to be impractical for life on the frontier. However, Mills and other reformers understood that Indiana needed to develop more than just basic farming skills if it was to progress beyond the pioneer era and toward a more advanced society and economy.

The debates over public schools and school funding in Indiana in the twenty-first century are eerily familiar. Every time Hoosiers today vote on a new school referendum, many of the issues with public education that troubled pioneers resurface. Citizens debate whether taxes are the most effective approach to balance the school budget as they consider the benefits and drawbacks of raising taxes to support public education. Some voters wonder if eliminating subjects they view as optional, like the arts, would have the same effect. Some parents teach their children at home because they dislike being told what subjects or schools their kids should attend. (Madison and Sandweiss)

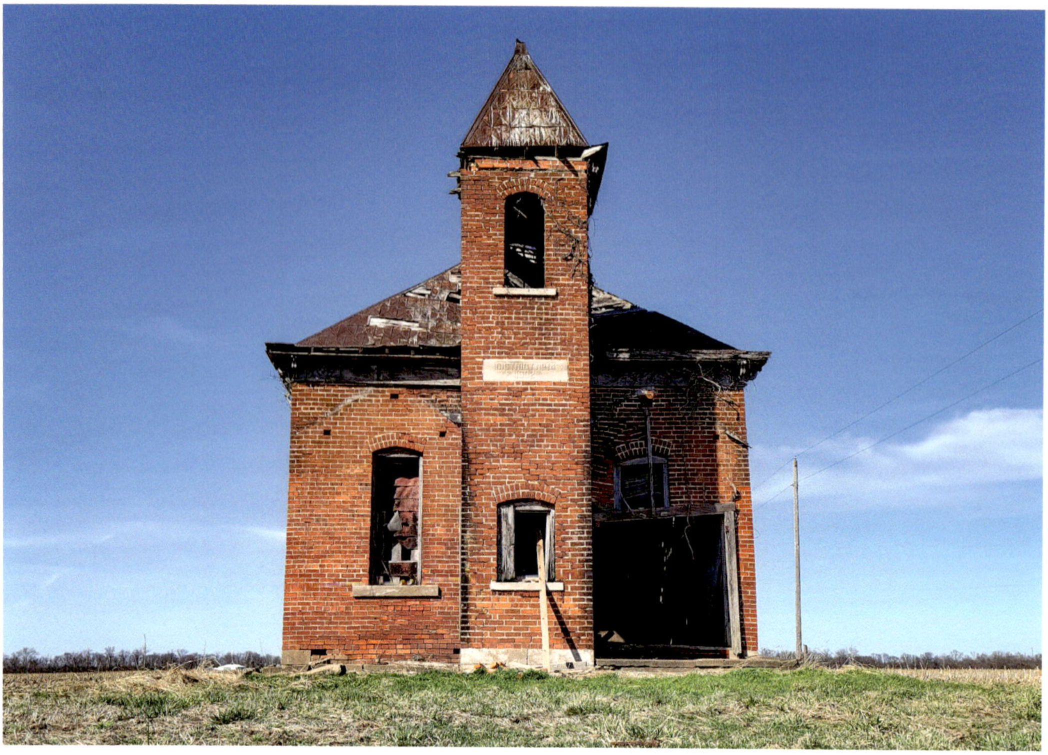

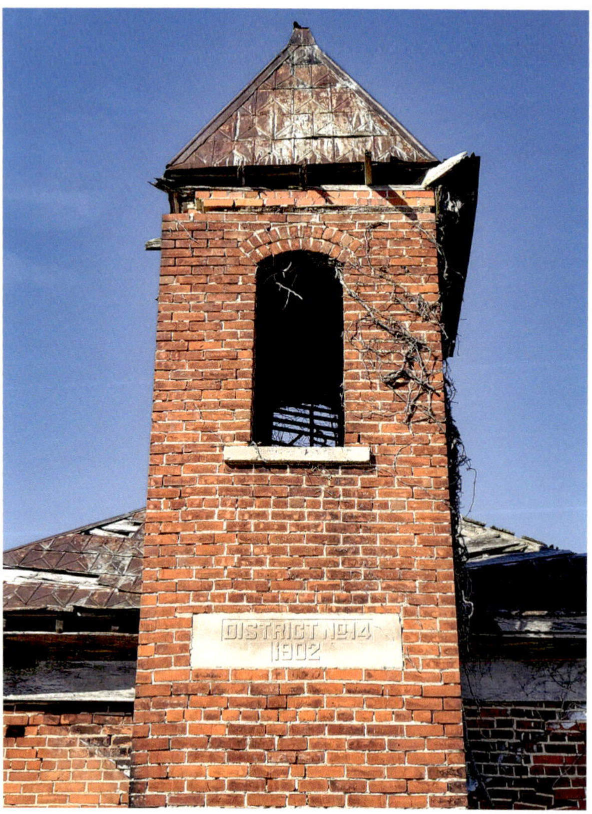

Above: District No. 14 School, built 1902.

Left: The tin roof has really held up over time. I'm a little disappointed that the bell was not left behind.

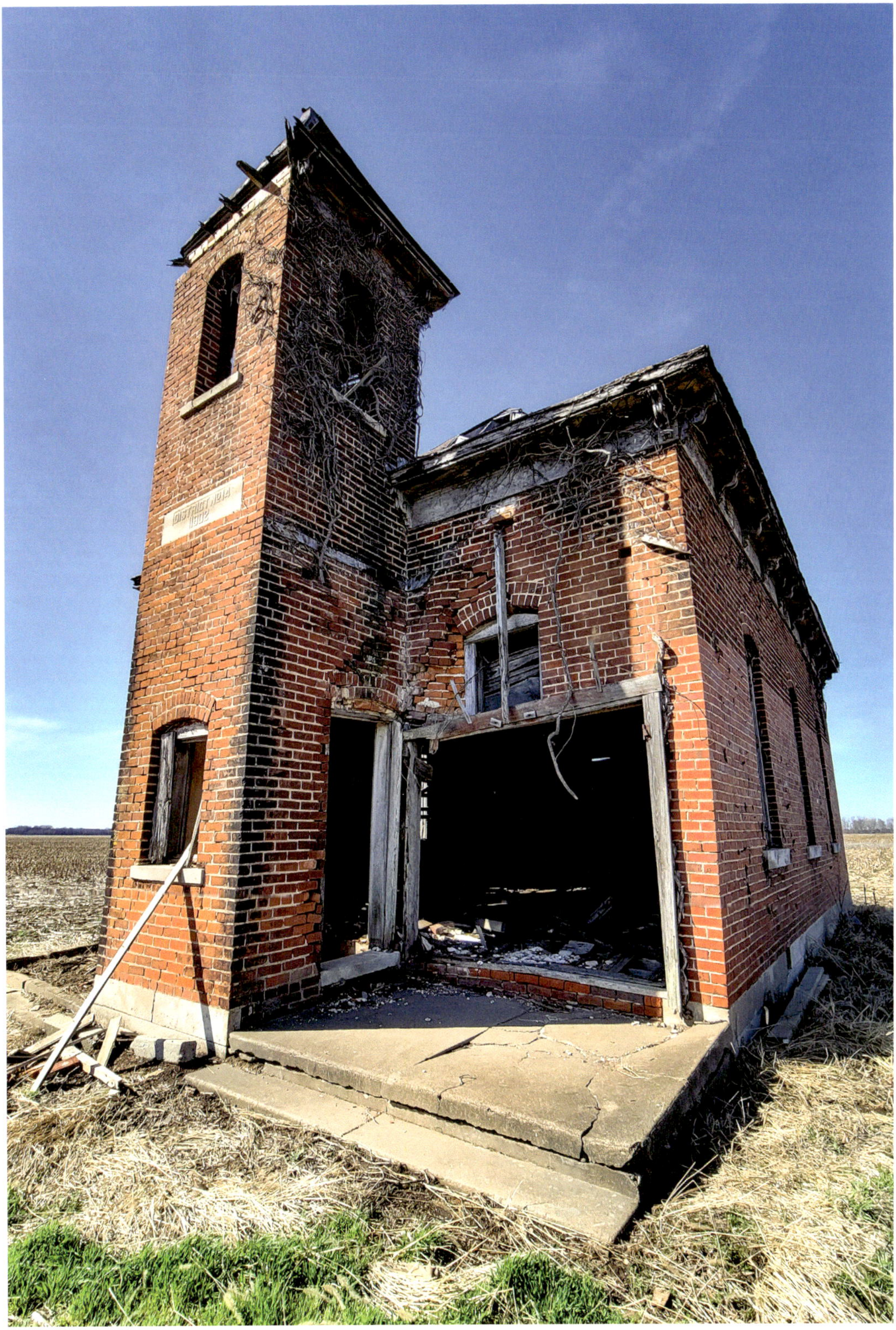

The school is in rough shape. A lack of maintenance has caused many of the bricks to shift and become loose.

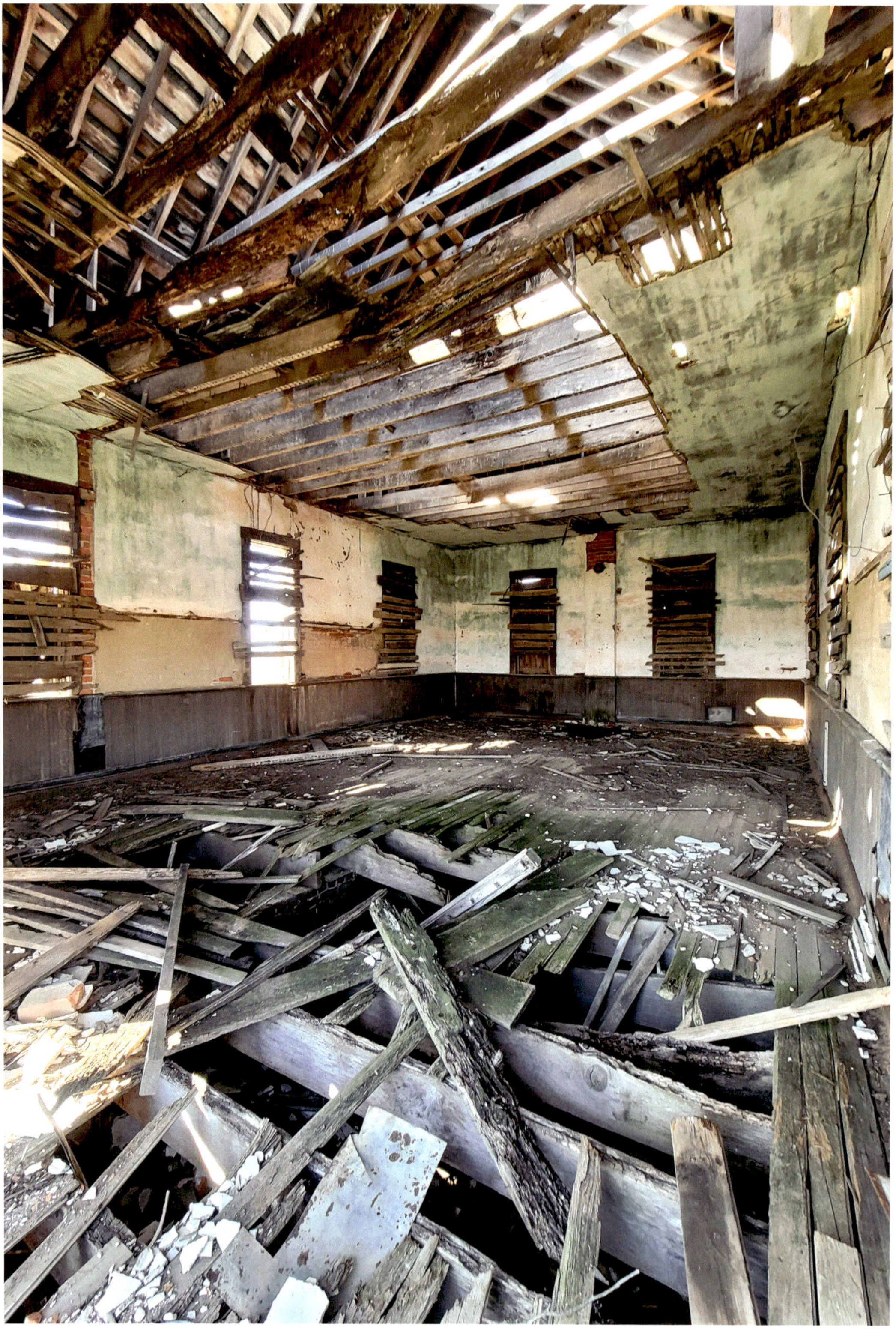

In one room of the school, half of the floor was completely gone, so it was unsafe to venture further.

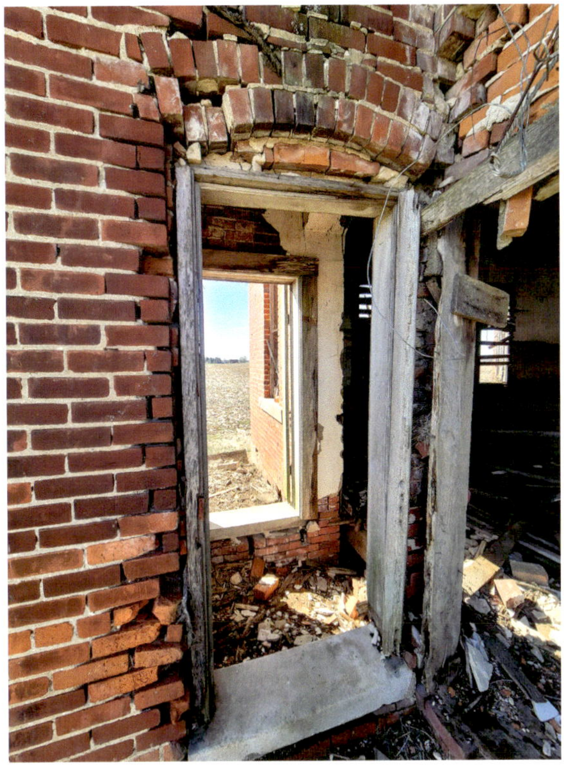

The bell tower and doorways, where the shift in the bricks is especially noticeable on the arches.

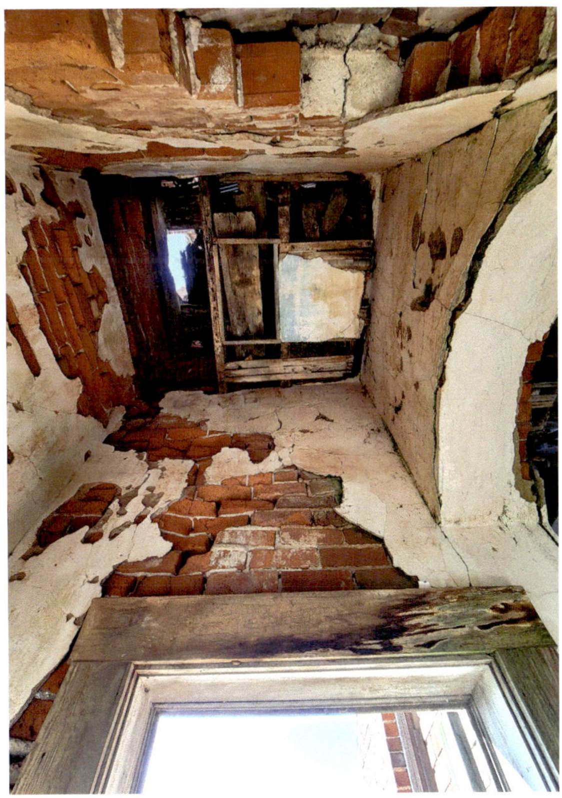

Looking up to where the bell would have been when the school was in use.

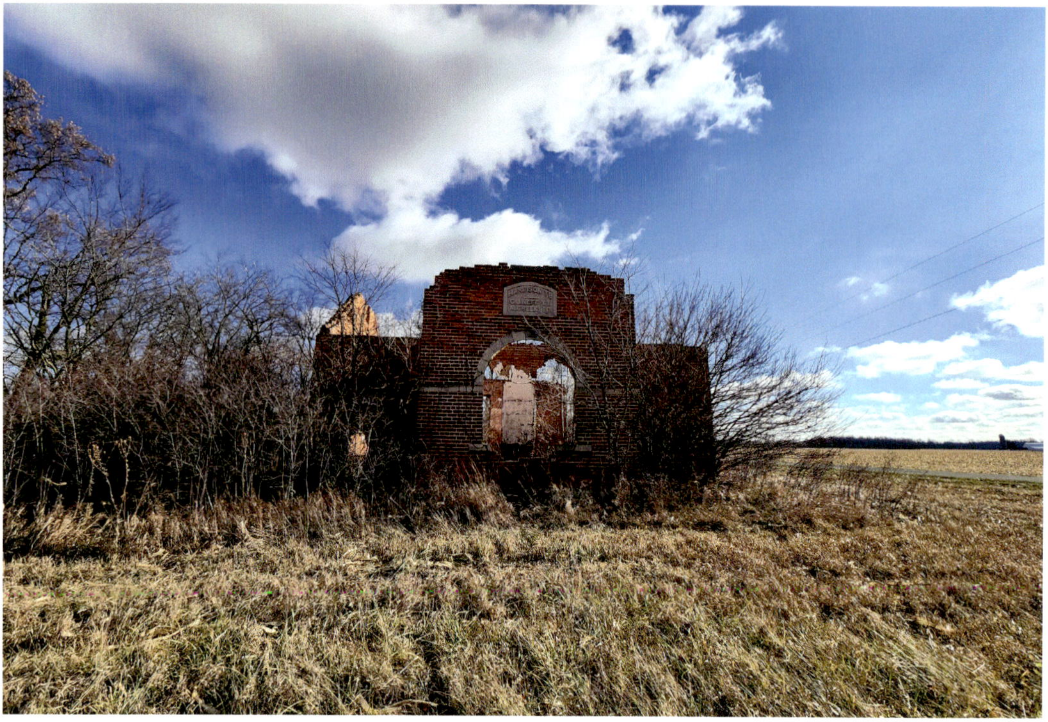

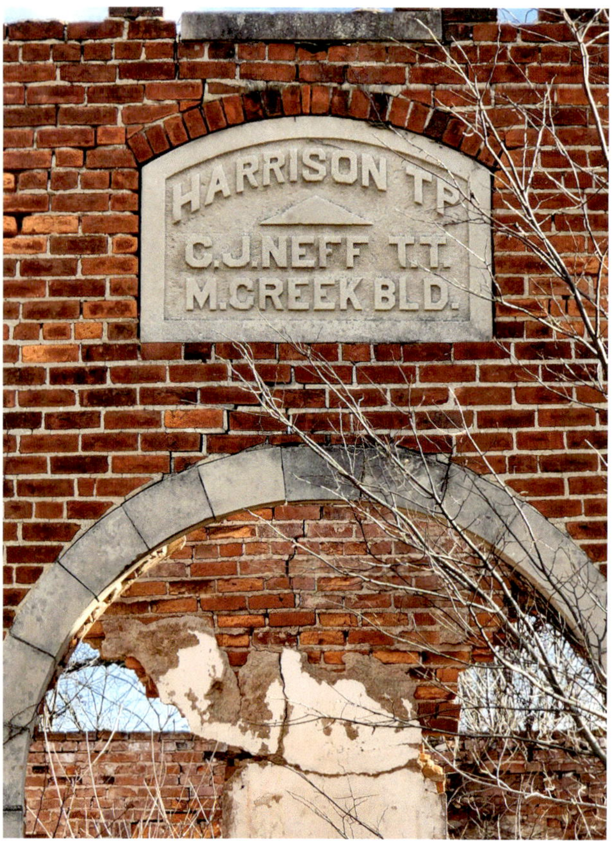

Above: Indiana is dotted with what remains of our history. Here we have the Harrison Township School

Left: The name plaque is in immaculate condition; you can clearly read the trustee and the builders' names.

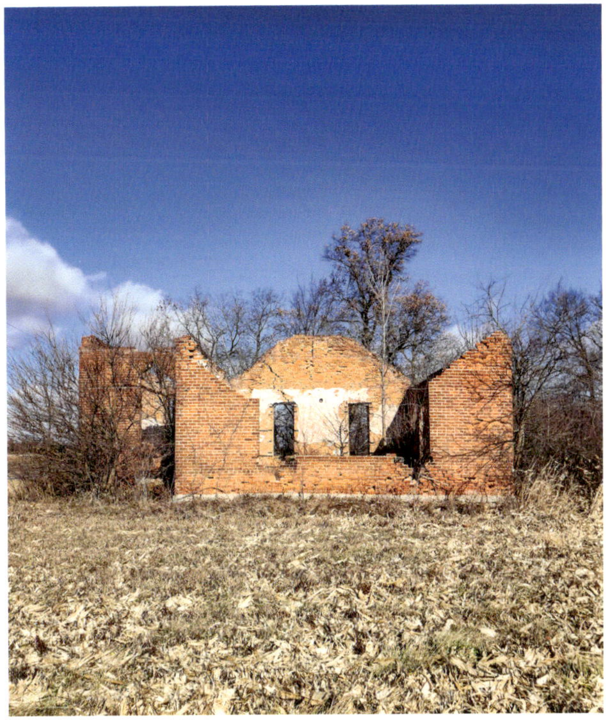

Right: Most of the school itself has collapsed, but a tree has made its home inside.

Below: The remains of the school as seen from the entrance.

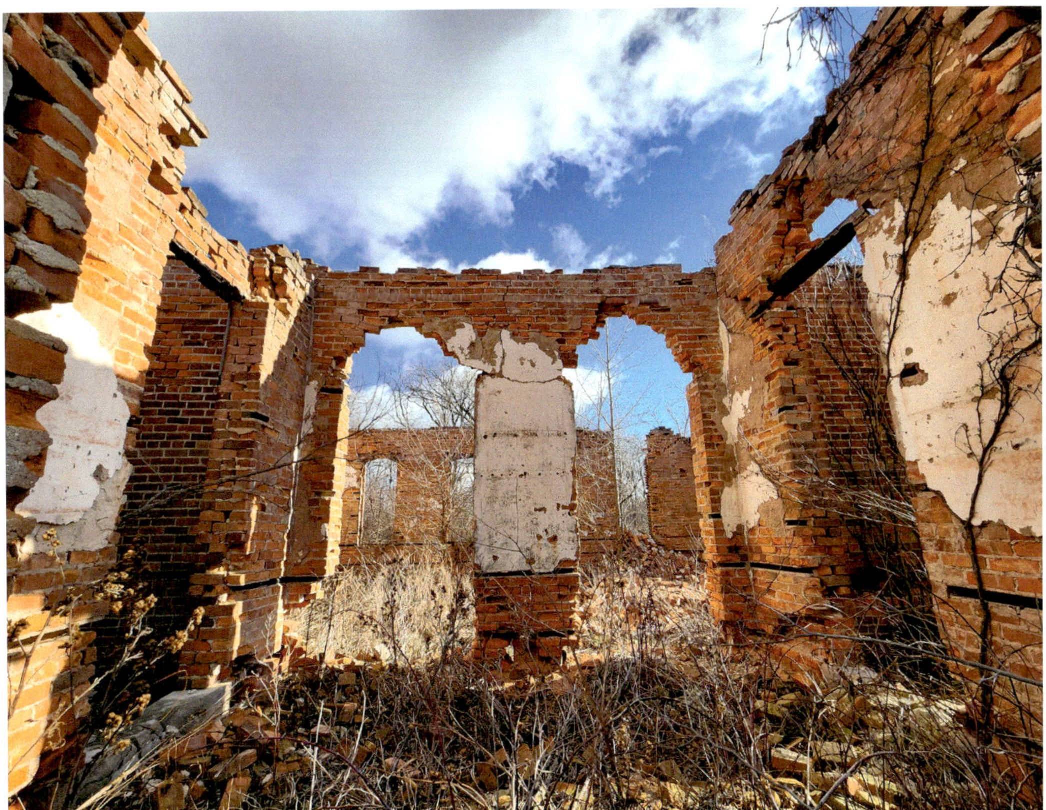

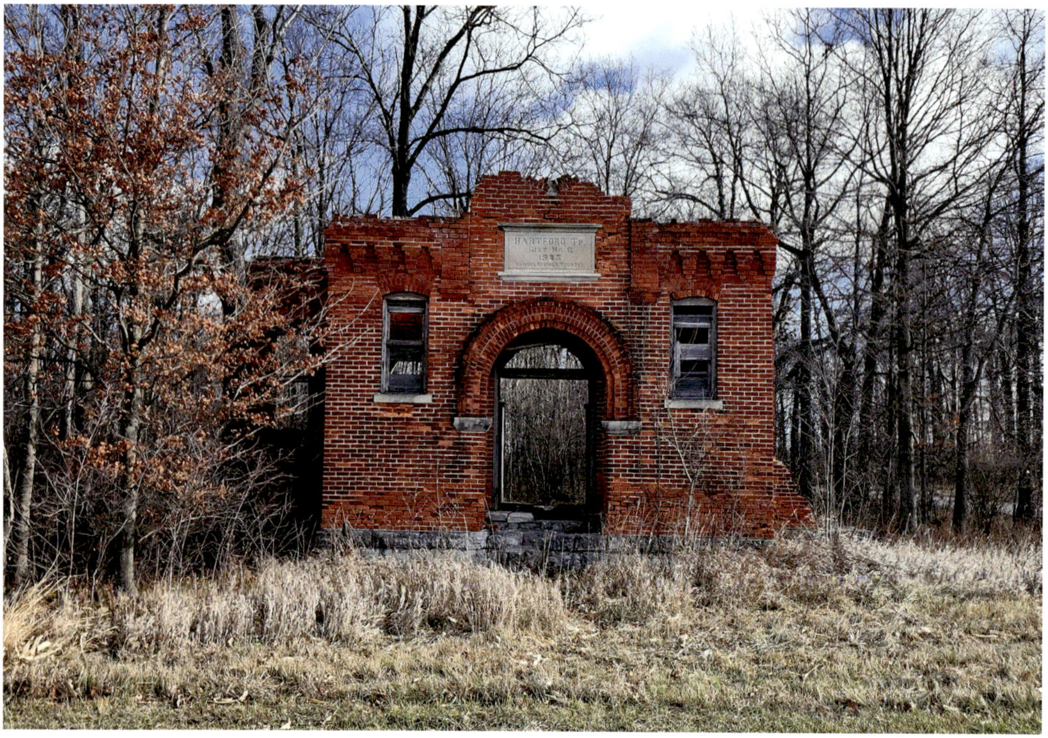

Hartford Township School; District No. 6. Trustee: Samuel Opliger.

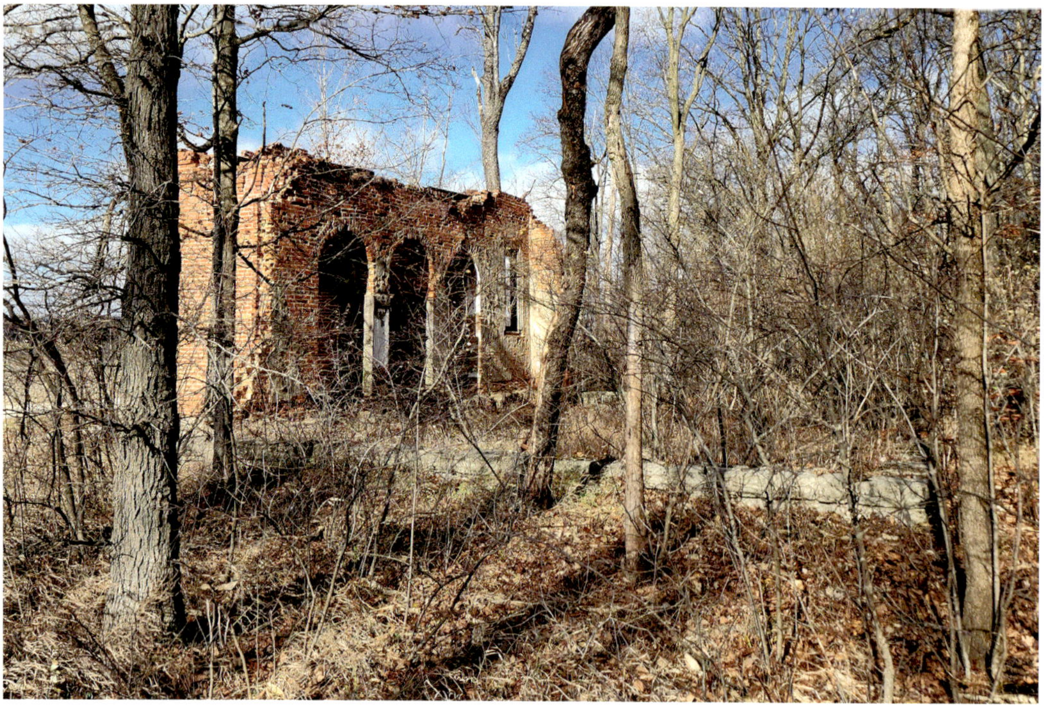

Over the years many of Indiana's old schools have been swallowed by the encroaching forest. The front of this one is completely intact, while the foundation is all that remains of the rest.

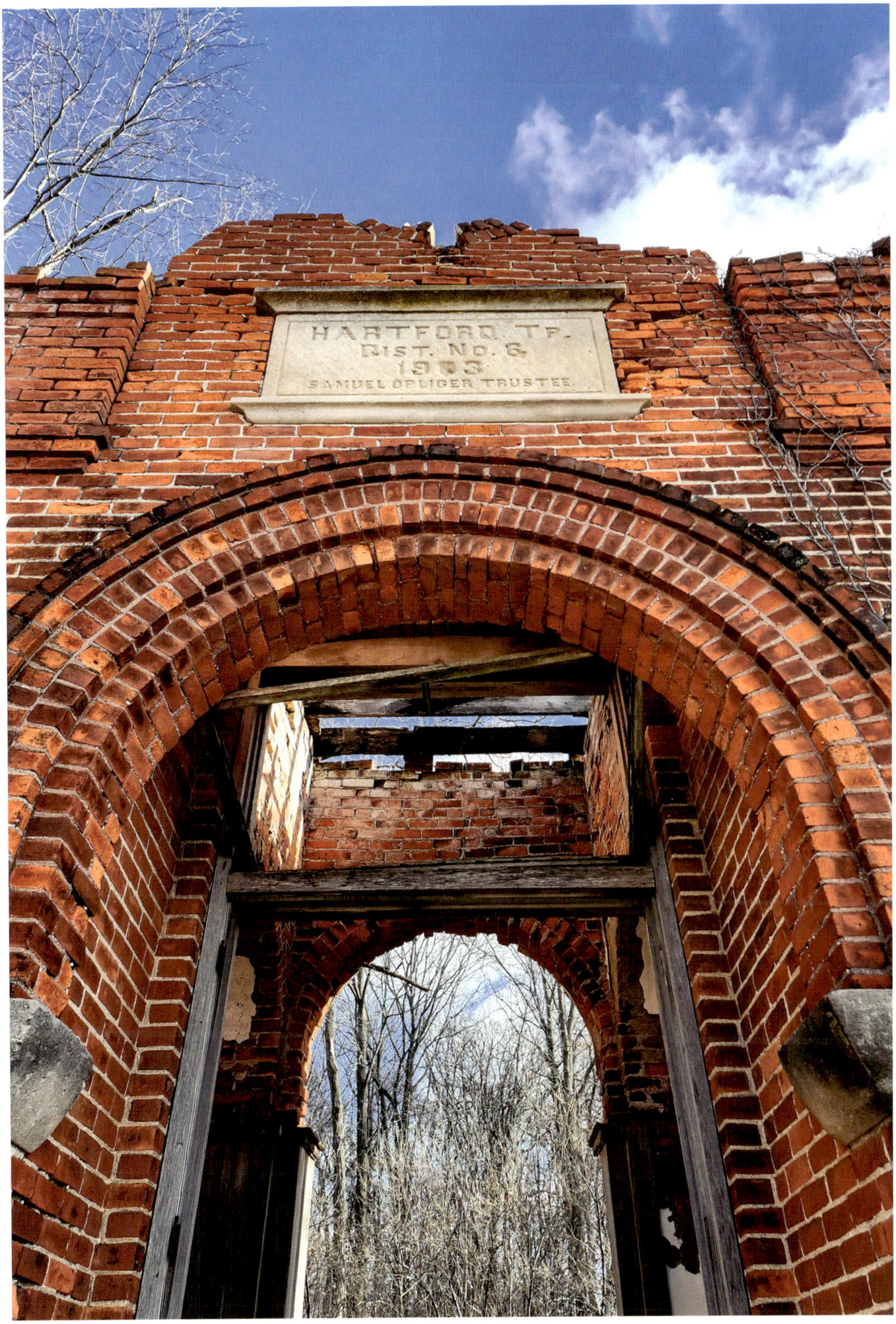

The entrance to the school, including the small open area where a bell would have been.

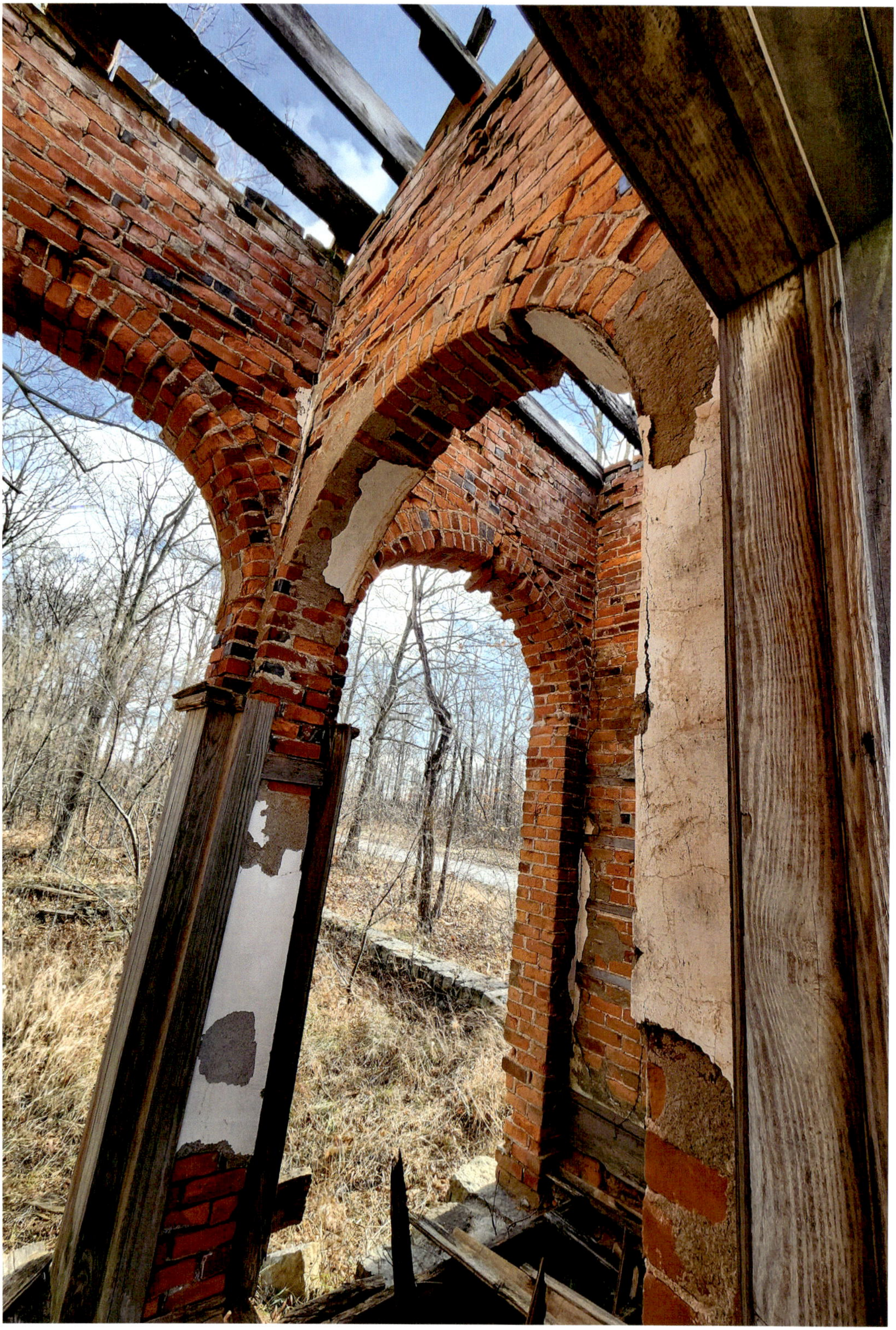

An archway in the entrance, looking onto the remains of the main room.

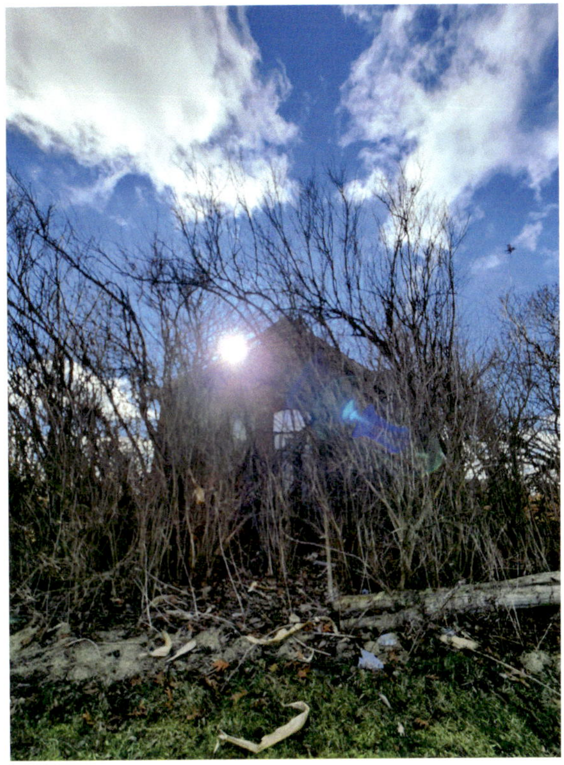

Many times, former schools were repurposed into homes, such as this one.

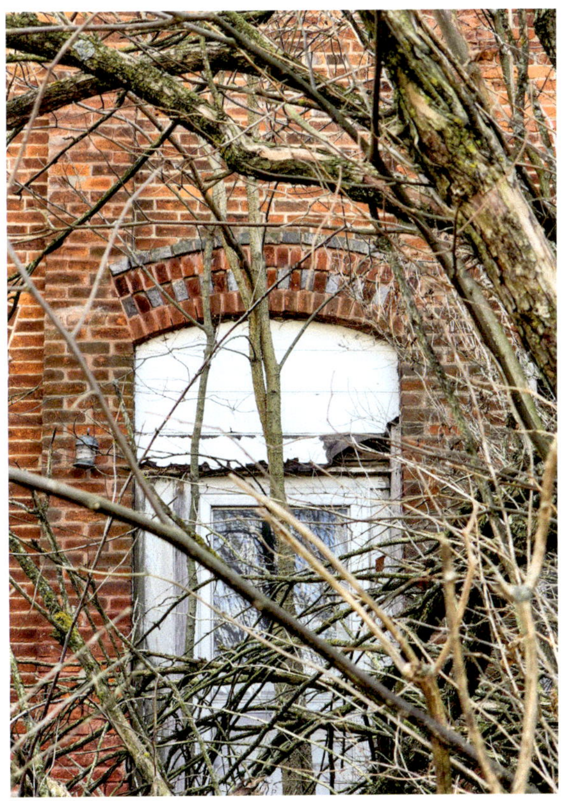

The corner stone is sometimes removed when that happens, but the light fixtures on this building were outstanding.

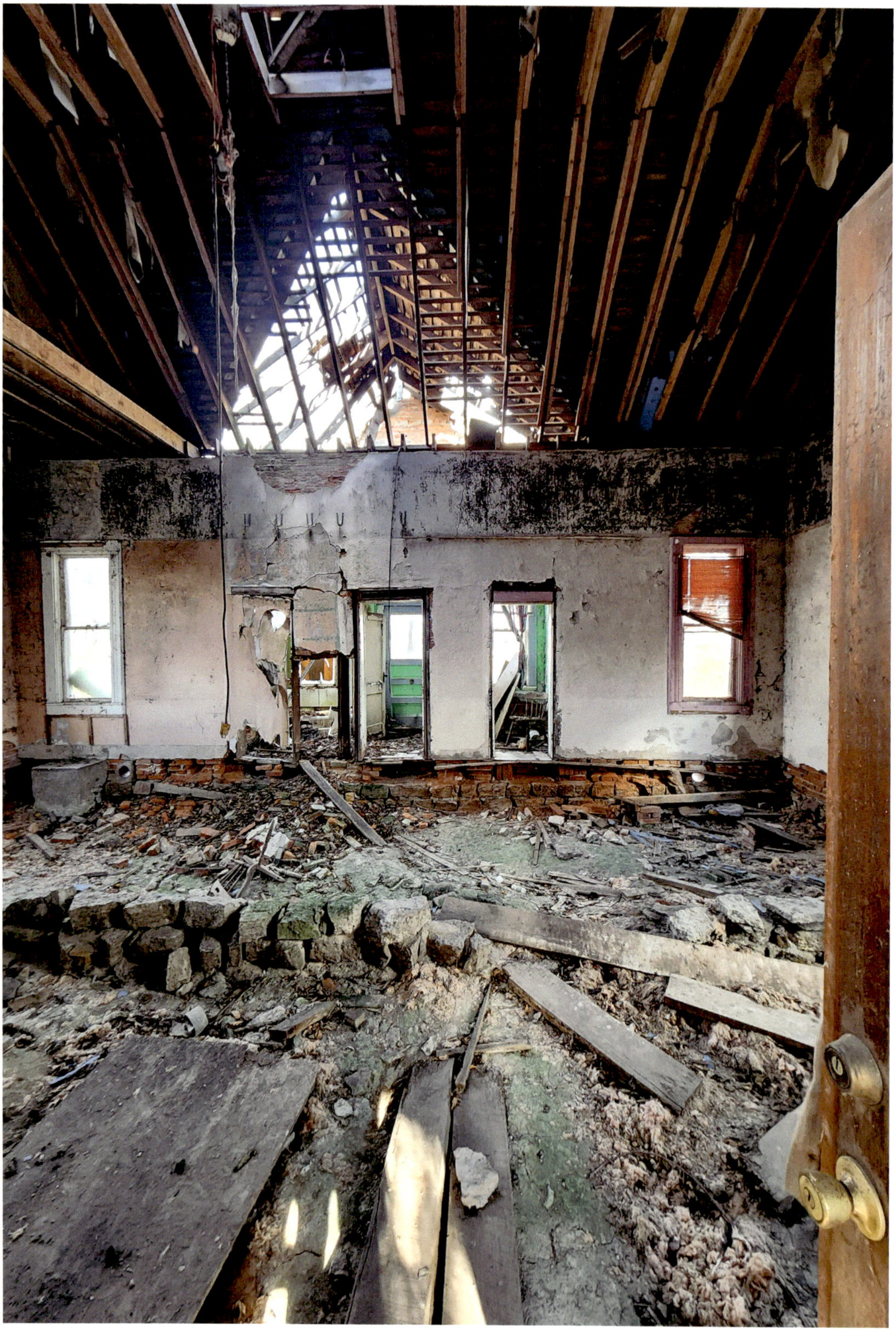

Inside, the building has been basically gutted, with large holes in the roof and the floor.

5

POPULATION BOOM AND EDUCATION AFTER WWII

Education has undergone the most substantial transformation of all state government responsibilities. The Indiana Constitution of 1816 stated admirable goals for public education but lacked the authority to carry them out. Laws that gave these intentions life only gradually developed. The pioneers and their offspring had to clear land, labor farms, and build roads because of their circumstances; they never put the constitution's progressive system into practice. The divergence, or gaps, in educational quality between urban and rural schools became more pronounced by the late 1950s; city schools provided wider curricula, teachers with more advanced degrees, contemporary school facilities, and extracurricular activities like music, theater, and sports teams. After years of discussion, Indiana's general assembly adopted the School Corporation Reorganization Act, also known as the school consolidation bill, in 1959, making it one of the state's most important pieces of legislation of the twentieth century. Small township schools were amalgamated into larger consolidated schools under the 1959 statute. In 1968, there were 382 fewer school corporations, down from 939, and more than 90% of Indiana students were enrolled in consolidated districts with trained administrators. Greater effectiveness and more consistent standards frequently reduced school identification, which decreased a sense of community pride. Old basketball championship medals in a glass cabinet in a brand-new merged school called "North Central" or "Eastern" felt out of place.

State funding rose along with the amount of state control over schools. During the Great Depression, local taxes made up the remaining 70% of school funding, with the remaining 30% coming from a state gross income tax. Up until 1973, when a property tax freeze caused the proportions to change, the state contributed roughly one-third of the school funding. Early in the twenty-first century, the state was funding education to the tune of three-fourths. Education has been at the top of the priority list for recent governors. Governor Robert Orr worked hard to implement his A+ education plan in the 1980s, which included making the school year 180 days long and introducing Indiana Statewide Testing for Educational Progress. (Madison and Sandweiss)

Early in the twenty-first century, Indiana had established one of the country's more egalitarian systems for allocating funding to schools, with less inequality between richer and poorer school districts than most states. However, critics persisted in claiming that the state did not invest as much in education as it might or should given that it spent less on public education than the national average, with the exception of higher education. Achievement discrepancies persisted, with children from affluent neighborhoods outperforming those from inner-city schools and many rural regions on standardized examinations. The impact on rural communities was especially hard. Health disparities, acute poverty, and food insecurity are problems in rural areas. Due to a lack of state and federal funding, schools are also obligated to act as food banks, hospitals, and daycare centers. Rural schools frequently served as both the center of a community's culture and its major local employer. However, because of these additional costs, rural school districts frequently experienced financing issues. While consolidation may give communities the prospect of a better education, they also lose a vital social hub, which ultimately leads to depopulation of these areas. (Secondo)

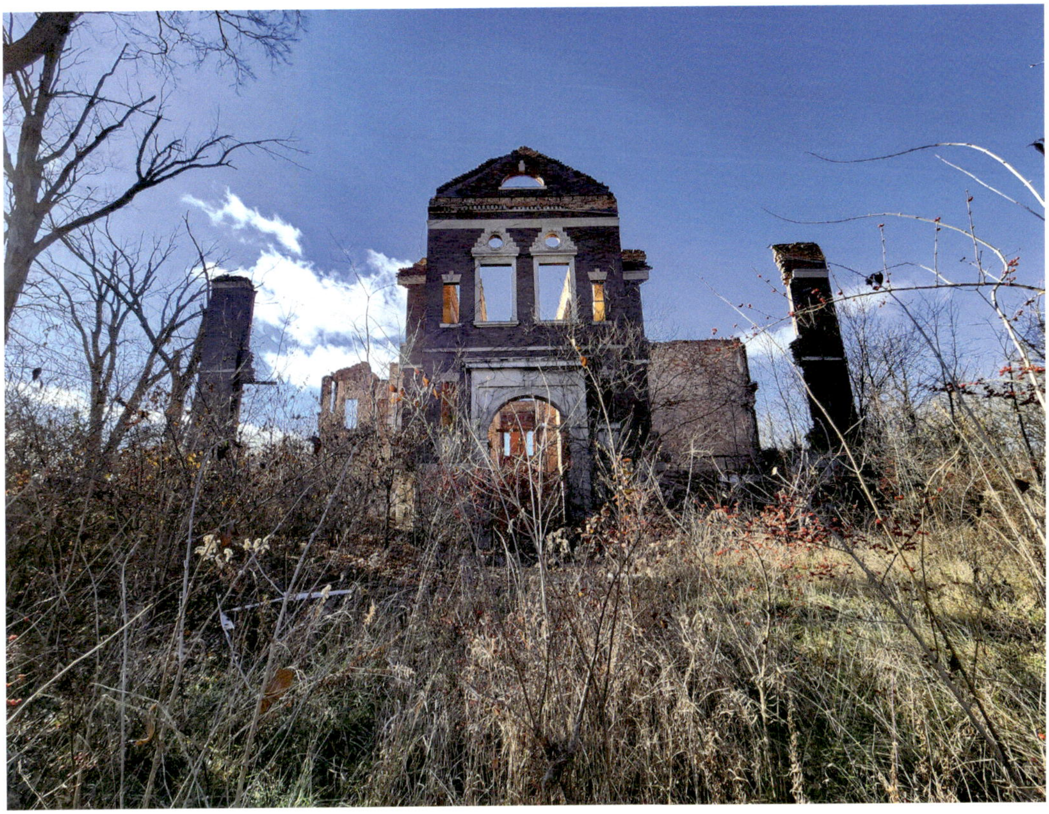

Above: Walking through a ton of plants and refuse to get to this school was completely worth it.

Right: The front of this school has the beautiful art deco details still intact.

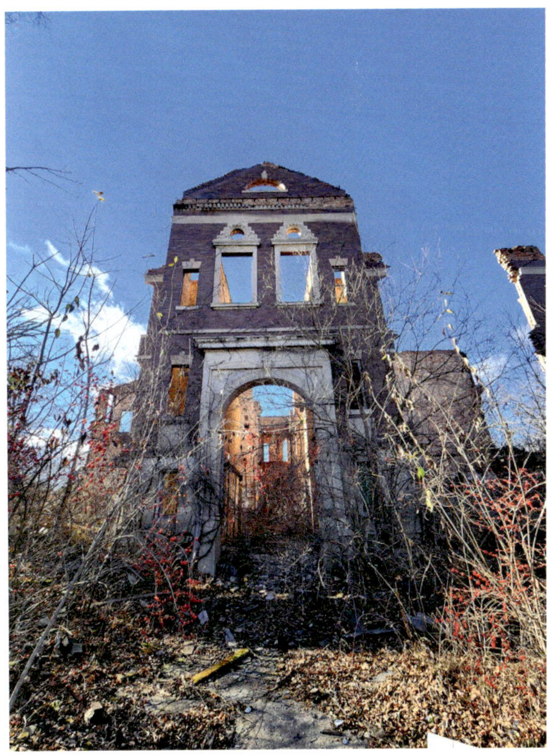

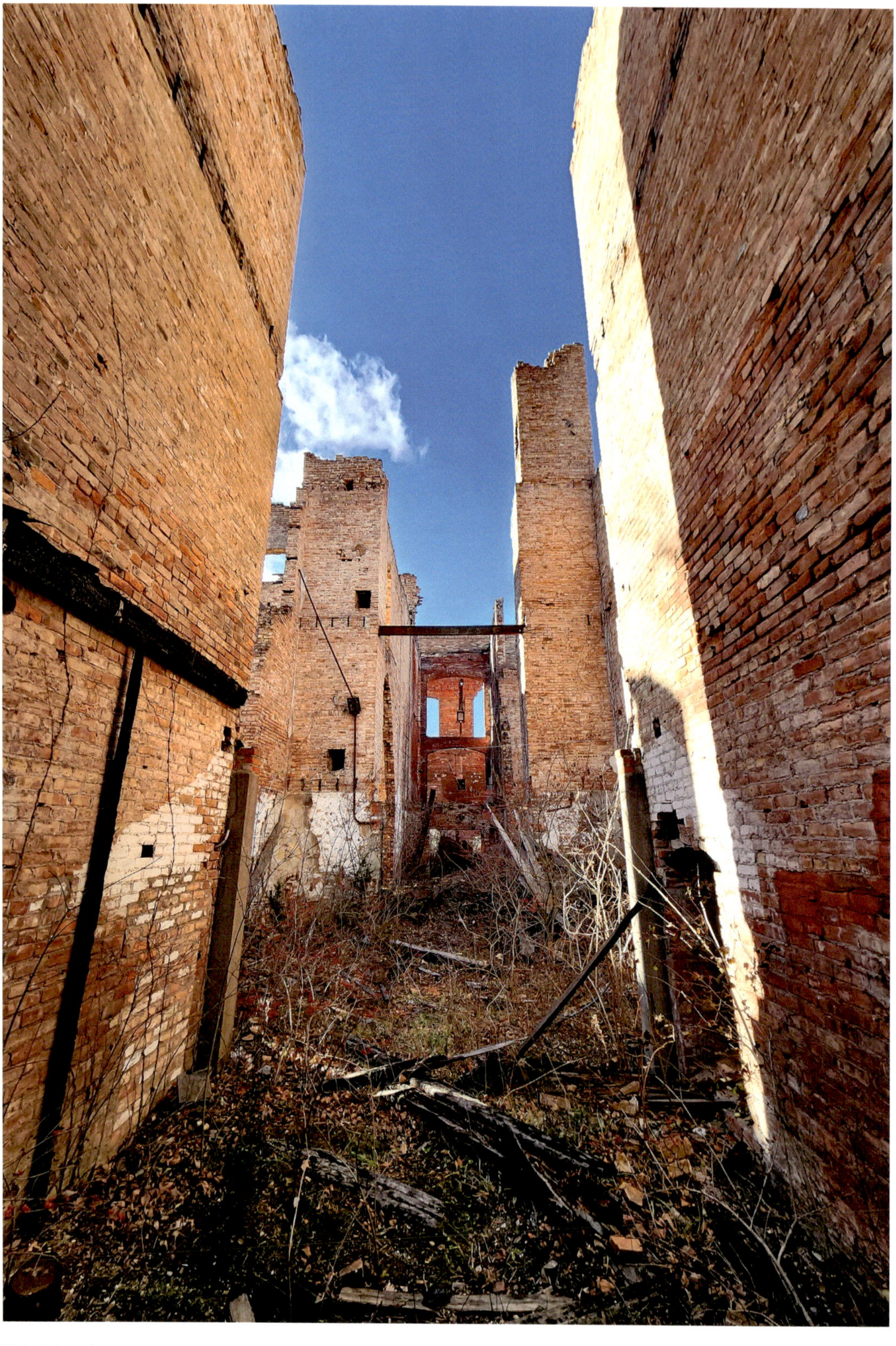

This is hands down one of the most breathtaking places we have ever found.

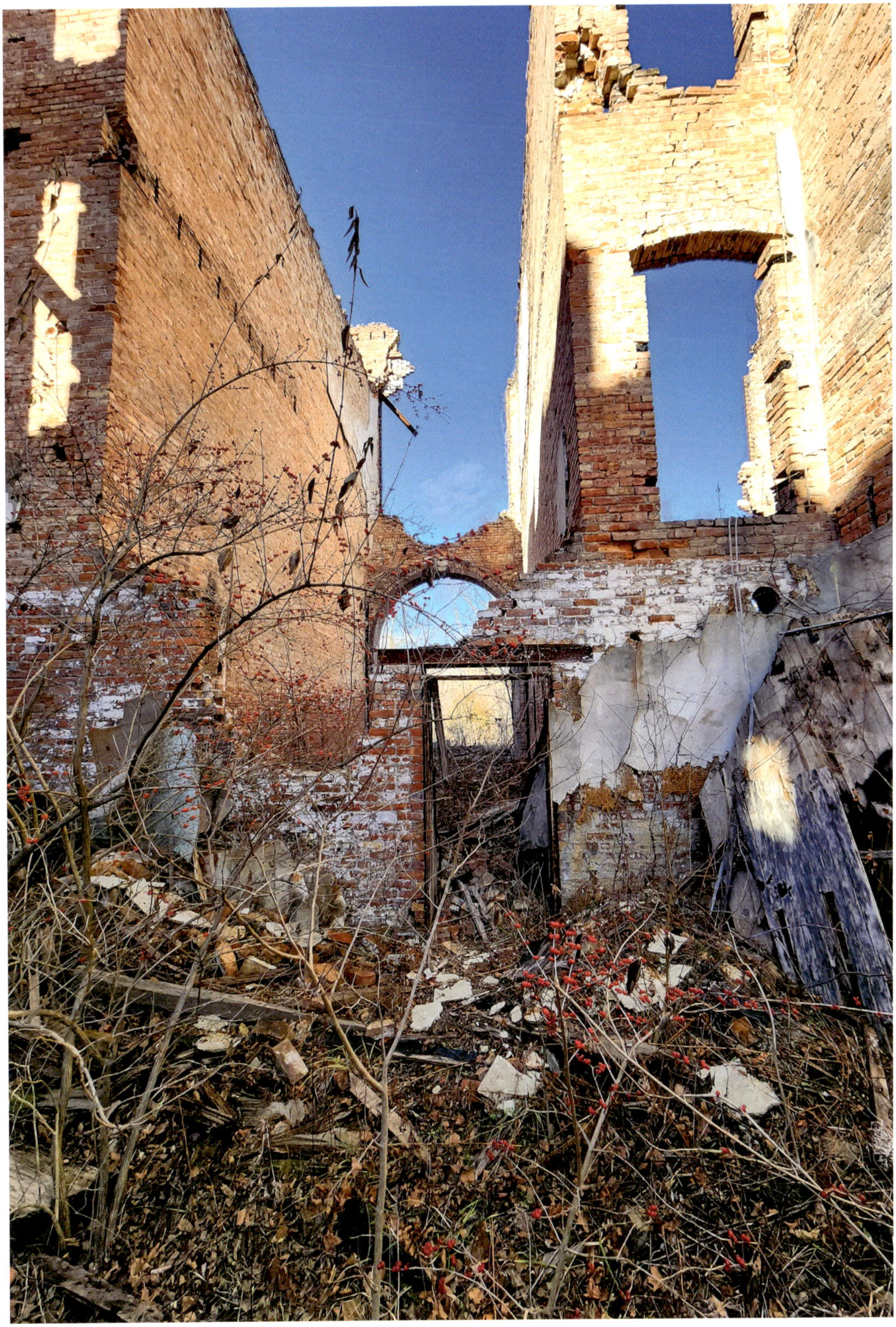

There had been a fire here at some point, but everything was very stable.

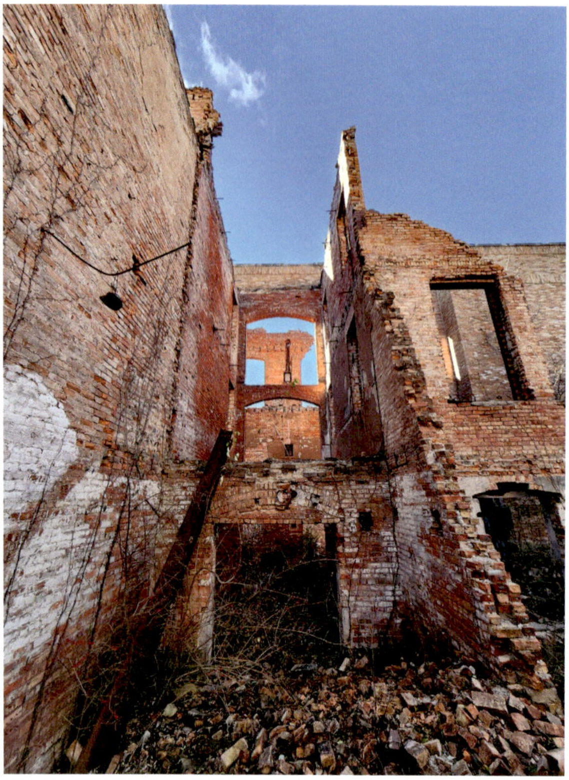

I really enjoyed finding light fixtures still hanging precariously.

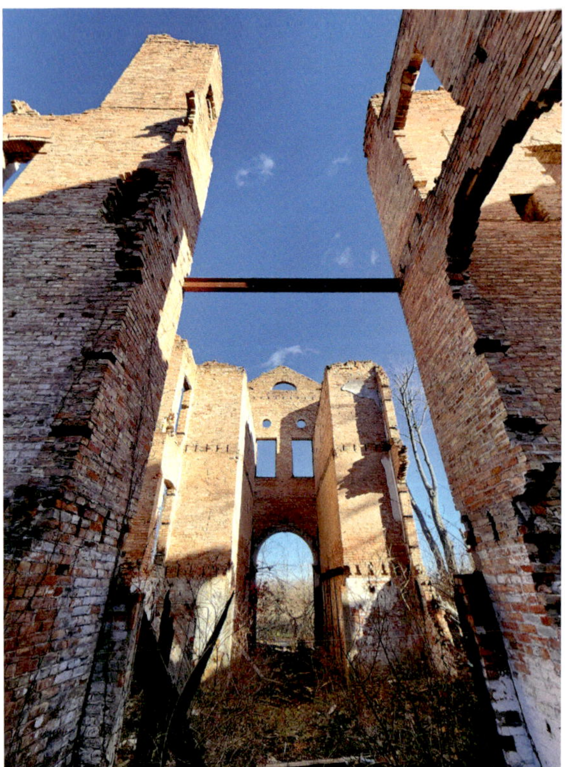

The front facade as seen from approximately the middle of the building.

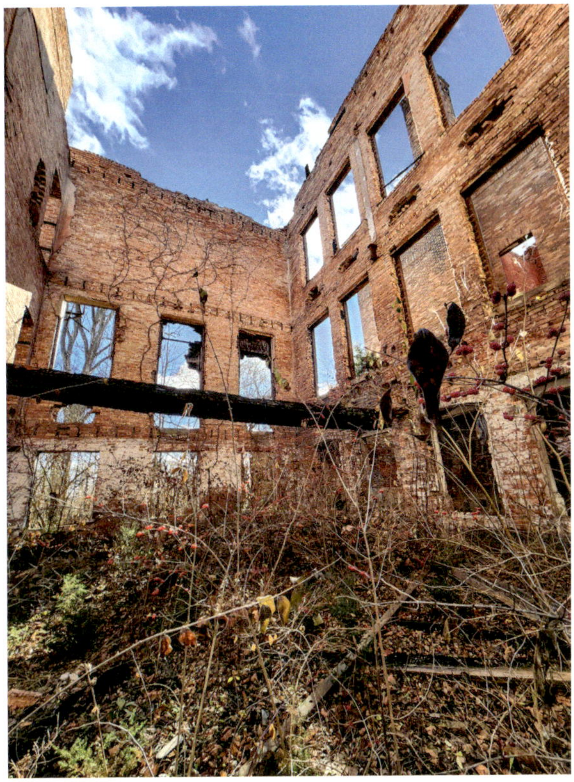

Most of the charred support beams were on the floor. This was one of the few that was still "supporting."

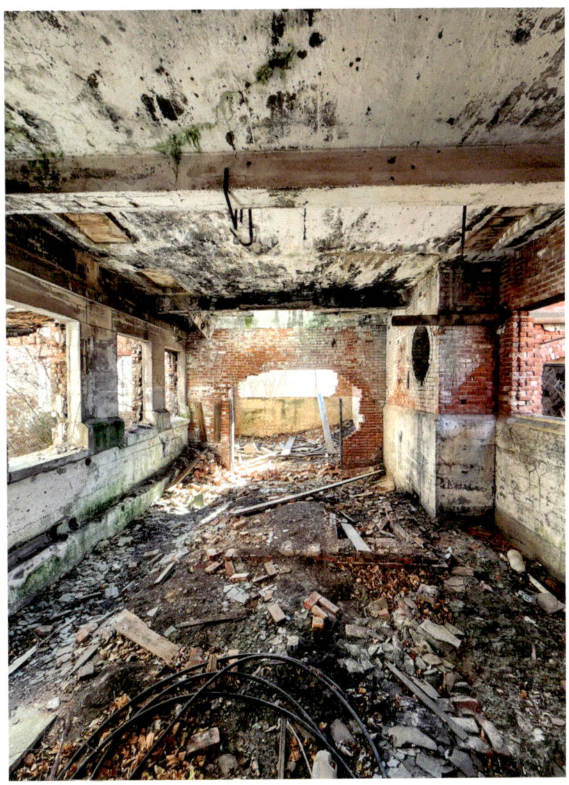

The basement level, most likely where the boilers and electrical supplies were kept.

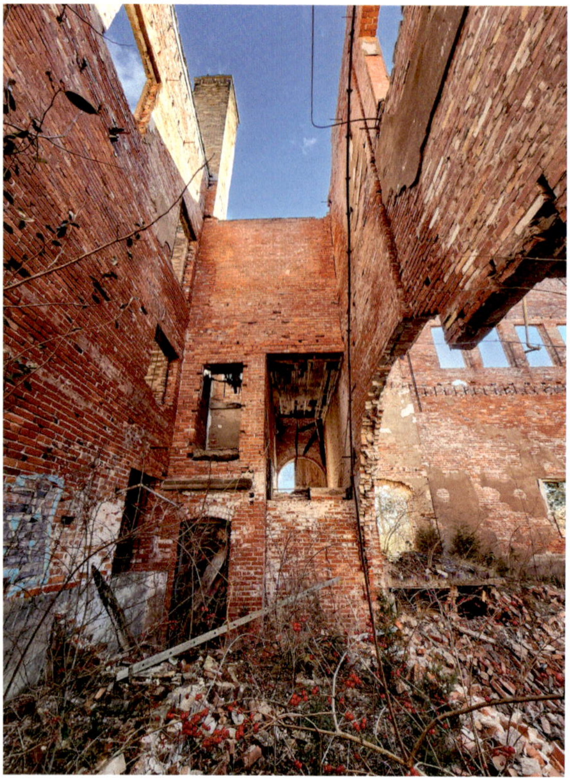

Looking up into the second-floor hallways.

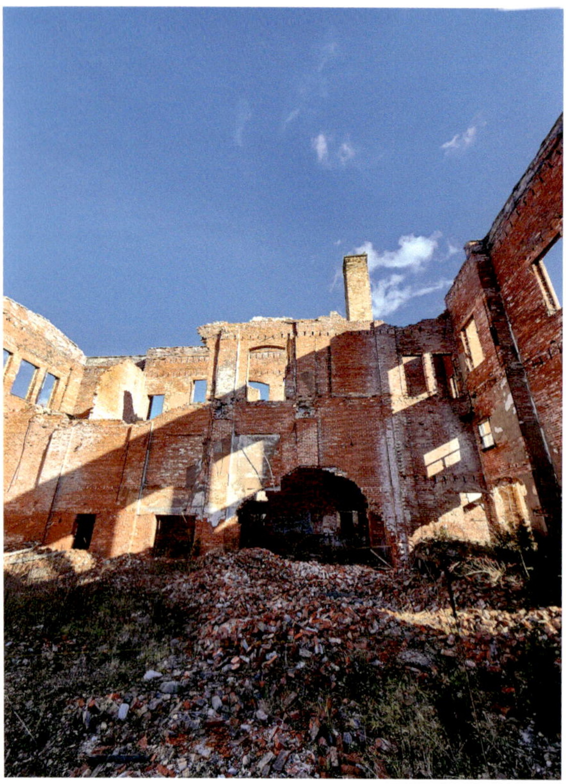

Due to the size of this room, it was most likely the gym/auditorium.

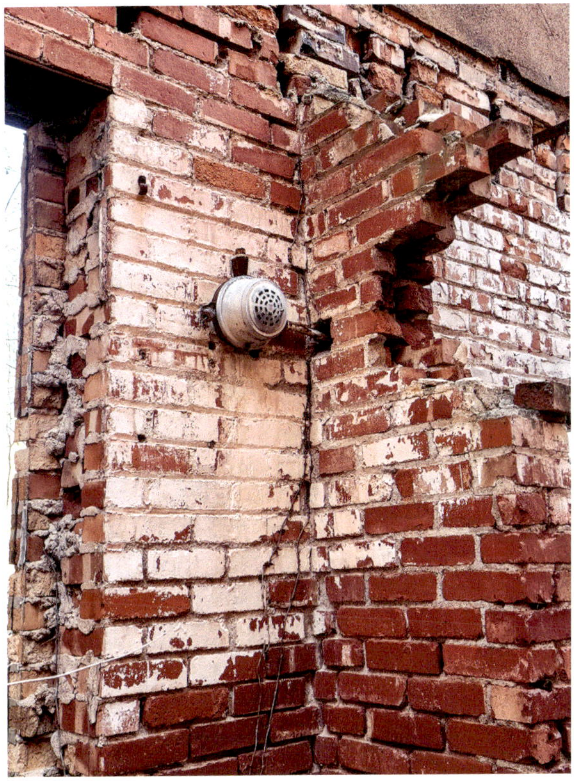

The announcement speaker still hooked up on the wall.

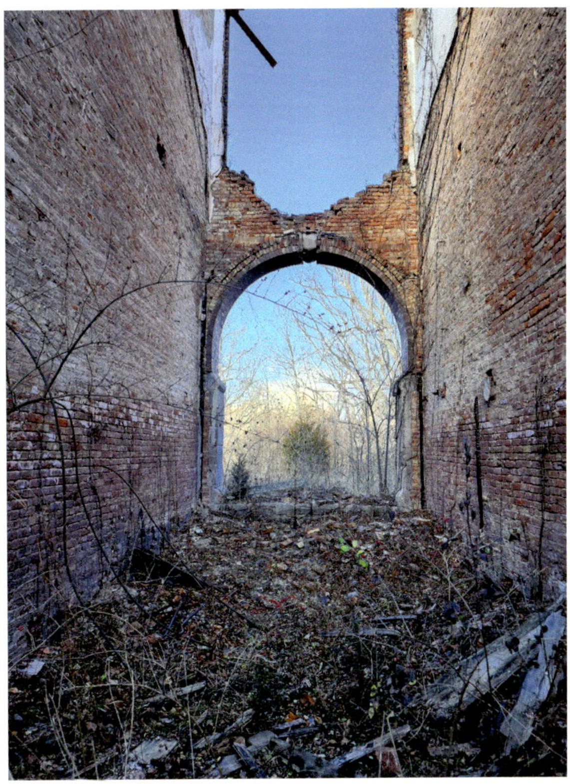

This arch looks directly into the surrounding forest.

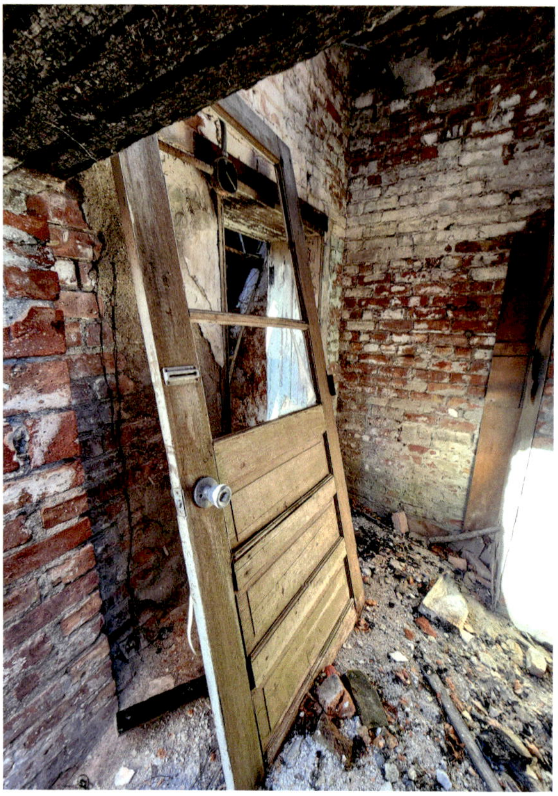

One of the very few intact hallways, including a door with a slide lock.

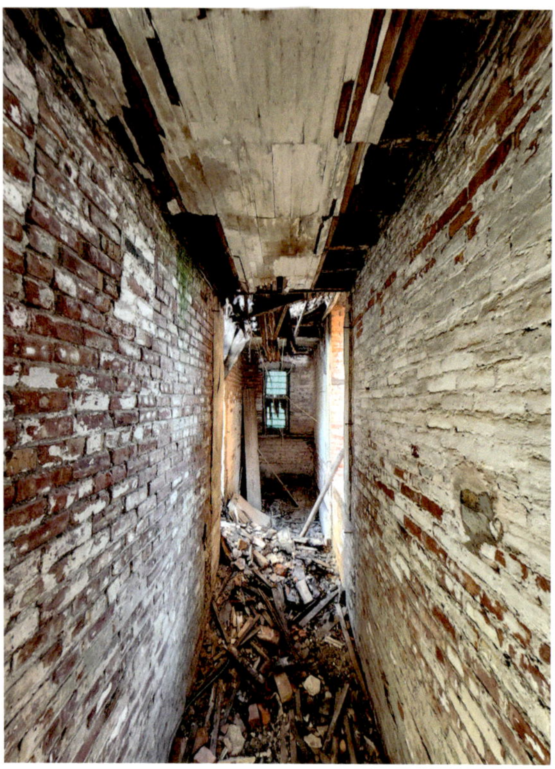

The end of the hallways had a beautiful blue window.

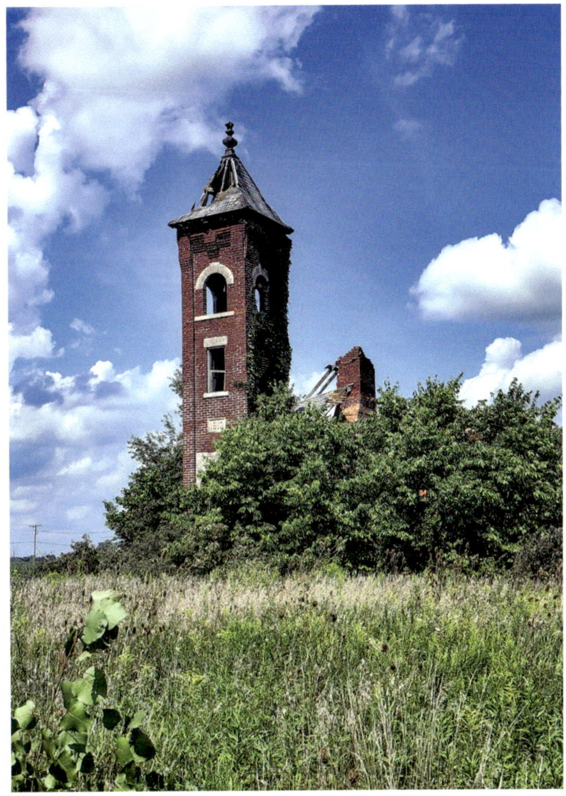

The remains of this school sit in the middle of a cornfield; luckily, it's tall enough that you can see it from the road in the summer.

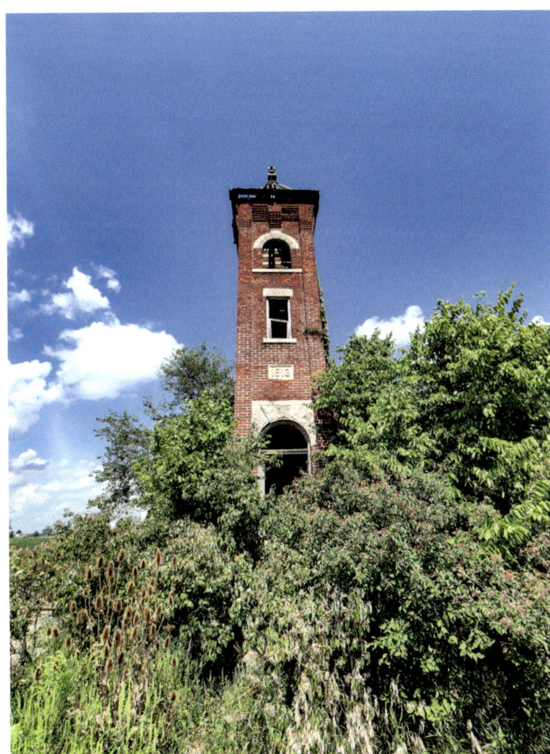

The bell tower sits empty. The doorway is incredibly high off of the ground since the stairs have long since decayed.

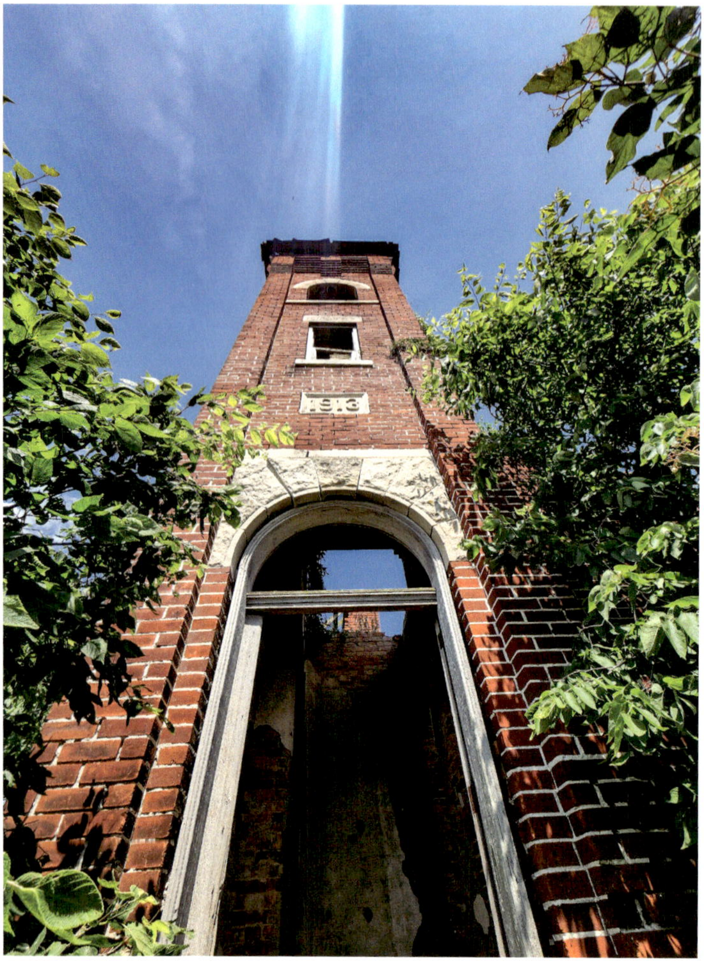

Left: Doorway and bell tower as seen up close. The main floor is approximately 4 feet from the ground.

Below: Inside the entryway, much of the floor is completely gone, and so are the walls.

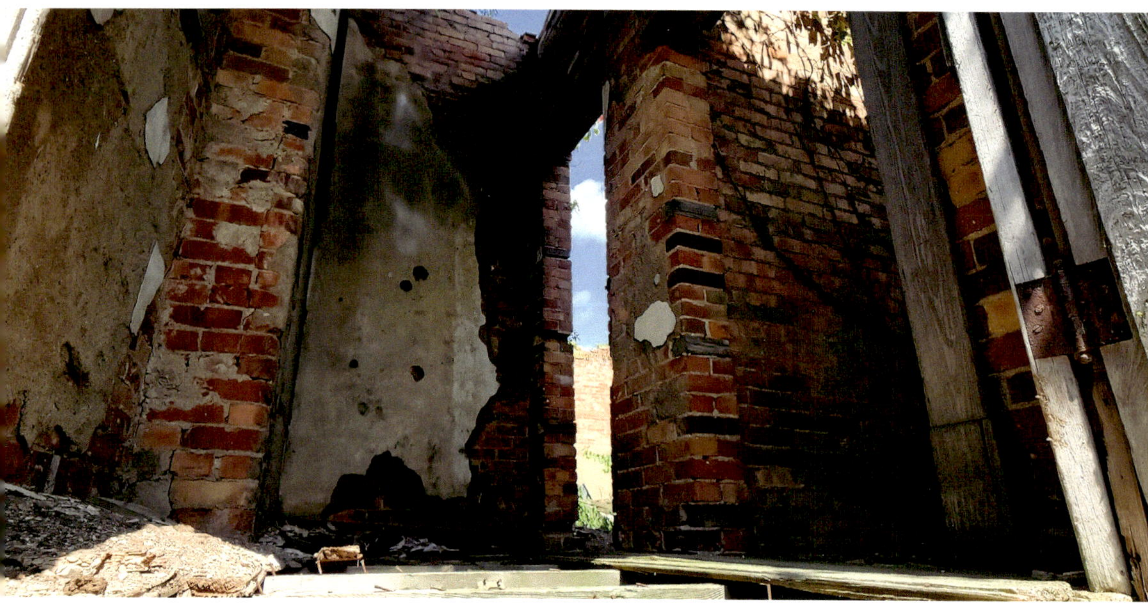

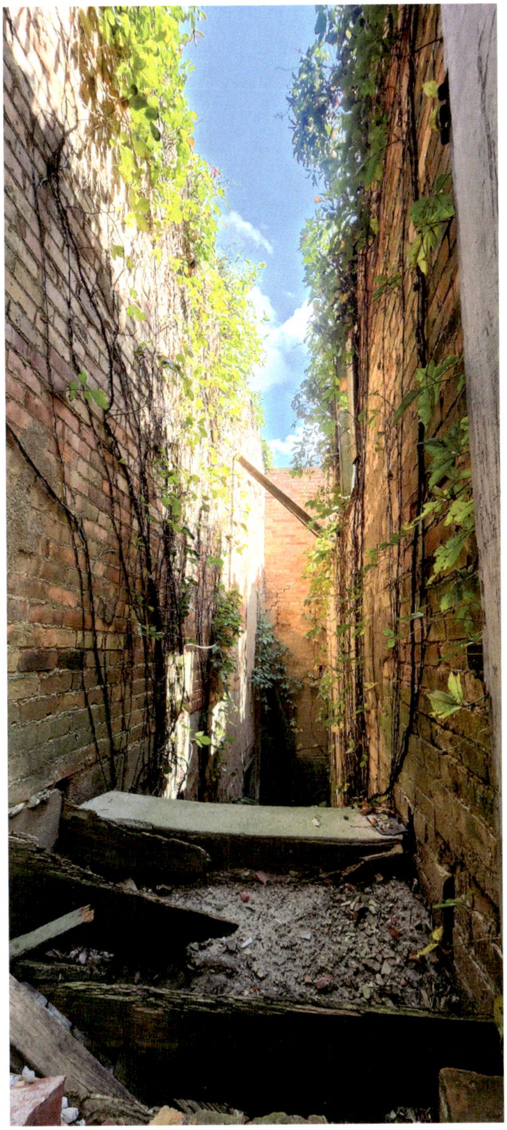

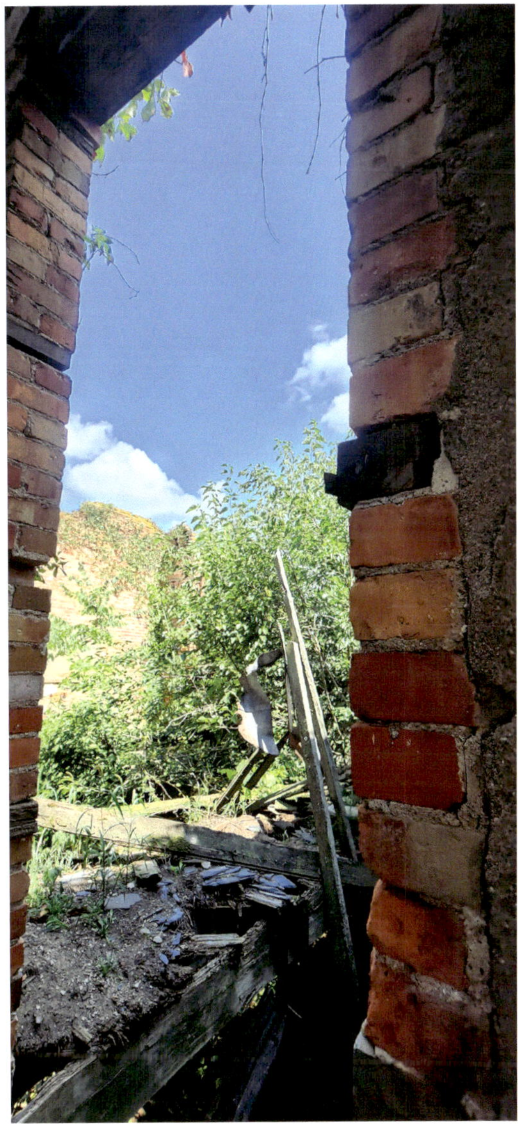

Above left: One of the hallways that would have led to a classroom. Nature has long since reclaimed it.

Above right: Looking towards the back, the wall gives an optical illusion of Indiana having any sort of mountain.

REFERENCES

Arnold, Melissa. "Indiana Scenic Drive: National Road." HowStuffWorks, 20 Mar. 2007, adventure.howstuffworks.com/scenic-drive-in-indiana-historic-national-road-ga.htm.

Bragg, K. B. Technical Report and Project History Contract NOy 5475. United States Navy.

Cierzniak, Libby. "The Crumbling Crossroads of America." 19 Sept. 2015, historicindianapolis.com/the-crumbling-crossroads-of-america/.

"Grissom." Air Force Civil Engineer Center, https://www.afcec.af.mil/Home/BRAC/Grissom.aspx. Accessed Oct. 2022.

Higgins, Will. "Indiana's 'Broken Arrow' — That Time 5 Nuclear Bombs Caught on Fire." *The Indianapolis Star*, 13 Dec. 2018, www.indystar.com/story/entertainment/2018/12/13/indianas-broken-arrow-time-5-nuclear-bombs-caught-fire/1831690002/.

Madison, James H., and Lee Ann Sandweiss. *Hoosiers and the American Story*. Indiana Historical Society, 2014.

National Park Service. "GRISSOM AIR FORCE BASE, BUILDING NO. 143 (Grissom Air Force Base, Water Survival Training Pool) Peru Miami County Indiana." Historic American Buildings Survey Midwest Regional Office, tile.loc.gov/storage-services/master/pnp/habshaer/in/in0400/in0452/data/in0452data.pdf.

Rademacher, Steven E. "Remedial Action and Final Radiological Status, 1964 B-58 Accident Site, Grissom Air Reserve Base, Bunker Hill, Indiana." Aug. 2000, apps.dtic.mil/dtic/tr/fulltext/u2/a381508.pdf.

Secondo, Noah. "Rural School Consolidation Is Not the Answer." *Harvard Political Review*, 25 Aug. 2020, harvardpolitics.com/ruralconsolidation/.